VOICE FOR HIRE

LAUNCH AND MAINTAIN A LUCRATIVE CAREER IN VOICE-OVERS

By Randy Thomas and Peter Rofé

Senior Editor: Amy Vinchesi

Project Editor: Stephen Brewer

Production Director: Alyn Evans

Published in the United States by Watson-Guptill Publications,

an imprint of the Crown Publishing Group, a division of Random House, Inc.,

New York.

www.crownpublishing.com

www.watsonguptill.com

Library of Congress Control Number: 2008934812

ISBN: 978-0-8230-9946-7

First Edition

Printed in the United States

1 2 3 4 5 6 7 8 / 15 14 13 12 11 10 9 8

CONTENTS

FOREWORD

By Don LaFontaine

Don LaFontaine is one of the most famous voices in promos today. You have heard his voice in hundreds of movie trailers, in Geico Insurance commercials . . . in fact, you hear him just about any time you sit down in a movie theater or turn on the radio or TV.

Scenario number 1: You're one of those guys with the deep, rich bass/baritone voices that set the women all atwitter. It commands attention. You're always being asked to play Santa at Christmastime. You make James Earl Jones sound like a ten-year-old girl. You get the idea. . . .

Scenario number 2: You're a woman with that appealing, sort of hoarse Demi Moore sexy kind of voice. You say hello to a guy and he offers to buy you a condo. You can make ordering a pizza sound like an invitation to spend the night. . . .

Scenario number 3: You're a person of either gender with that guy/gal next door, all-American, white-bread, "Honestly, would I lie to you?" kind of voice. Butter actually melts in your mouth. Total strangers would trust you with their children. . . .

Scenario number 4: You have that urban, ethnic, "street" kind of delivery. Even if you're dressed in a powdered wig and silk pantaloons, you would be mistaken for a rapper or a New York cab driver. You don't sound anything like one of those announcer people. . . .

Scenario number 5: You don't fall into any of those categories. You're just somebody who is interested in trying to break into the voice-over game.

Could you, in all of the above cases, make a go of it?

Well, sure. But, not without a little guidance. Fortunately for you, that guidance comes from people who are well qualified to provide it: the first female to announce the Academy Awards and New York's most highly sought-after voice-over coach. I could say that Randy Thomas and Peter Rofé have forgotten more about this business than most voice artists will learn in a lifetime, but they haven't forgotten a thing, and this book proves it.

Believe me, it's a minefield out there. Like any other form of show business, 5 percent of the performers do 95 percent of the work, and the remaining 95 percent divvy up the 5 percent that's left over.

And that's how it should be. When advertisers are counting on you to persuade the public to buy their products, they want to be sure you can deliver. In a very real sense, an entire industry can rise or fall, depending on your ability to sell their wares.

But, no pressure!

Virtually anybody who can speak clearly can succeed in the voice-over world. Some might be limited by regional or foreign accents, or by having a voice that is too specific or unusual, but there is work for anybody who is willing to take the time to develop his or her ability. And that's where this book enters the picture.

Here is a step-by-step guide to help you put your feet on the right path. What you will learn in these pages is critical to your understanding of how the business works, and how you can best prepare yourself to work in the business. You will learn how to develop your talent and to maximize your vocal quality. You will be taken inside the business to see how it works, and how the people who operate within it think. In short, it is a map through the minefield.

Don't leave home without it!

And don't stop here. Since the key to a successful career in voice-over is reading, read everything about this business that you can. The more you know, the better prepared you will be. Believe me, you are going to need all the help you can get.

Good luck. Really, I mean it.

ACKNOWLEDGMENTS

It is from the deepest place in my heart that I thank all of the students with whom I have worked, and all of the voice-over artists who have so generously shared a slice of their unique experience within these pages. Don LaFontaine, thanks for writing our foreword and for setting the bar so high. In the dictionary under the term *consummate pro* you will find Don's picture.

I also owe gratitude to:

The best agents any girl could have. On the East Coast, the Atlas Talent family: Lisa Marber-Rich, Jonn Wasser, John "Hoss" Hossenlopp, Ian Lesser, Marilyn McAleer, Rachel Sackheim, and David Lyerly. On the West Coast, my agents at TGMD in Los Angeles: Steve Tisherman, Vanessa Gilbert, Kevin Motley, and Ilko Drozdoski.

All the other agents who had a hand in helping build and shape my career.

Gil Cates, Don Mischer, Jeff Margolis, Gary Smith, Louis J. Horvitz, Jim Tanker, Ricky Kirshner, and Glenn Weiss, for your belief in me and for letting me play such an important role in your live broadcasts.

John Shanahan for not being reticent (inside joke) and Dr. Thelma Reese, for your friendship, guidance, and inspiration.

Leslie Kallen, for being an awesome literary agent and encouraging me to write.

Walter Anderson, for your advice, encouragement, and support.

Caryn Clark, for your insight and editing in the home stretch, and my lifelong friends Debbie Ford, Arielle Ford, Diane Weiss, Randie Knoblock, and Kevin Gershan.

Peter Rofé, you are twice blessed. First, with your beautiful wife, Bonnie, and then with your daughter, Sophie, your best production to date. Thank you for letting me share in the love.

Also, thank you to my family: Terry Thomas, Robert and Maria Stember, and Teddy and Susan Stember. I am so incredibly grateful for all that we have endured and transcended and for the memories of our brother Ronnie and Poppy. It was those challenges that left us strong and resilient. And, a world of thanks to the Wohl family for your never-ending love and support.

And finally, thanks to my husband, the amazing and magical Arnie Wohl, and our daughter, Rachel. You are the center of my universe from which all things flow. Rachel, loving you is my most important job in the world. I love that you already know the power of your voice.

—Randy

This true labor of love would not be complete without thanking the following individuals:

Voice-over announcer and private client Steve Kamer, who introduced me to Randy Thomas.

All of the voice-over agents at Atlas Talent for believing in me as an artist, as a coach, and as a producer.

My former agents at CESD in Los Angeles and at Abrams Artists Agency in New York.

My personal sound engineer, Ryan Fagman, whose behind-the-scenes wizardry sprinkles the final dash of magic.

My former personal assistant, Jess McLeod, and my current right-hand man, Mark Turetsky.

Fred Miller, for his editorial advice.

Don LaFontaine, for summing up our book in less than two pages.

My parents, for their unconditional love and support over the years; my brother, Richard, who taught me how to be an entrepreneur; my sister, Jessica, who confirms my suspicion that there is a genetic link in the ability to nurture talent.

Randy, who inspired me throughout the years of coauthoring a book long-distance.

My gifted and committed voice-over artists who make up the PDR Voice Over Coaching family, and who make coming to the studio each and every day an absolute pleasure.

And a special thanks to Craig Colfelt, Liv Rooth, Becky Balsley, and Mort Crim for their permission to showcase their individual voice over reels on our instructional CD. Thanks also to voice artists Doug Turkel and Sonny Warner for their permission to use their master-class coaching sessions.

And finally, my daughter, Sophie, and my beautiful wife, Bonnie, whose endless love and support inspire everything I do.

—Peter

ABOUT THE AUTHORS

Randy Thomas

America's most recognizable female voice announcer, Randy Thomas has been winning accolades and opening doors for female voice artists for nearly fifteen years. Randy began her career studying acting with both HB Studios in New York City and Adam Hill in Los Angeles. With more than twenty years of experience as a radio personality in New York, Los Angeles, Detroit, and Miami, Thomas has gone on to achieve her dreams as a freelance voice-over artist.

She was the first woman to announce the Academy Awards, the Miss America Pageant, the Tony Awards, the Screen Actors Guild Awards, and the National Democratic Convention (2004, in Boston, Massachusetts). She has announced the Oscars seven times and is the first person ever to announce The Oscars, The Tonys, and The Emmys in the same year.

Randy is currently the voice of CBS Television Distribution's *Entertainment Tonight* and *The Insider*, two of the most-watched entertainment news programs in the world. She is also the voice for Clear Channel radio stations across the country, including WASH FM Washington, D.C., WNIC Detroit, and Clear Channel's top-grossing station, WLTW New York. She is well known as the voice of *Hooked on Phonics*, memorably intoning the line "Call 1-800-ABC-DEFG."

Peter Rofé

Peter began his career like many actors: searching for an honest way to earn a living while pursuing a life in the theater, which paid little or sometimes nothing at all. He has appeared in dozens of national commercials, ranging from Pizza Hut to Peppermint Patty. He has also found his way into the voice-over booth, where he has voiced hundreds of commercials, promos, narrations, video games, and audiobooks.

Peter owns and operates PDR Voice Over Coaching, a recording and production studio in Manhattan, where some of the highest paid voice-over artists hone their craft. He became one of the first adjunct professors to teach a voice-over class at New York University's Tisch School of the Arts Drama Department and has taught live interactive voice-over seminars as well as prerecorded podcasts for online voice-over services. He has also produced hundreds of high-end voice-over reels for his private clients, helping them land lucrative work in commercials, cartoons, video games, industrials, audio books, and narrations.

Peter resides in Westchester County, New York, with his wife, Bonnie, and daughter, Sophie.

PREFACE

This book is designed to teach aspiring voice artists, in a step-by-step format, how to break into an extremely competitive marketplace.

Neither of us subscribes to the belief that "this is the way you do it and that's that." Since we are all unique, with our own diverse voices, methods, and messages to convey, there cannot be a definitive right way or wrong way to approach this craft.

Even so, certain trends and truths can inform your career. We have created what we feel is a sensible approach you need to take to achieve your goals, along with insightful comments and stories from the voice-over industry's top agents, casting directors, producers, and, of course, artists.

We will help you open the door and stay in the room once you get there.

Part 1

Breaking Into the Business and Finding Your Voice

- **Where to Begin?**
- **Commercials**
- **Promos**
- **Narration**
- **Audiobooks and New Media**
- **Animation**
- **Live Announcing**
- **Trailers**

"Everybody needs coaching."

—Lisa Marber-Rich, Atlas Talent Agency

Where to Begin?

1

- The Qualities of a Good Voice-Over Artist
- Working with a Coach
- Joining a Class
- How to Choose a Coach or Class
- Exercise: Step Right Up to the Microphone

Voice-overs are much more a part of our daily lives than most of us probably notice . . . unless, of course, you are a voice-over artist. When we call to get movie times and listings we are greeted by an all-too-familiar voice intoning, "Welcome to Movie Phone!" In many of today's luxury cars, a recorded voice helps drivers navigate their chosen routes. Museum acoustic guides educate patrons as they tour exhibits at their own pace. Then there are movie and television promos and announcements, radio commercials, voice mail, online instruction, video games and DVDs, educational programming, cartoons, and books on tape. It's not hard to see why the demand for trained professionals known as voice-over artists is increasing.

WHY A BOOK ABOUT VOICE-OVER?

Men, women, and kids of all ages earn money using their voices. Many are members of the actors' guilds, the American Federation of Television and Radio Artists (AFTRA), and the Screen Actors Guild (SAG), and the nonunion work available out there is even more plentiful (the caveat is that nonunion work offers a lot less than professional actors get paid—some call it "dollar a holler"). The point is, there is work, and if you have the desire to try your hand at it, this book will be your guide. Even if you don't think you can handle the competition but love the idea of being more confident the next time you need to speak in public or read a bedtime story to your kids, this book will help you understand what's involved in using your voice effectively.

Back to those of you who are interested in exploring a career as a voice-over artist: We've designed this book to give you a grounding in the various areas of potential employment—commercials, promos, narration, audiobooks and new media, animation voicing, live announcing, and trailers—and solid, proven advice about how to approach them, including how to create a demo reel that producers will listen to, how to conduct a marketing campaign that will get you jobs, and how to land and work with an agent.

THE VOICE-OVER ARTIST

In everyday life, the experience of interacting with others is guided in many ways by our vocal presentation, and we each have within us different voices for dealing with life's daily opportunities and challenges. Your vocal pitch, modulation, tone, and intensity will differ considerably depending on whether, say, you are requesting a pay raise from your boss or attending a parent-teacher meeting. When you unexpectedly meet a friend on the street your tone is likely to be relaxed and friendly, while you may sound shrill and enraged when someone backs into your car in the parking lot.

> We have become convinced that the human psyche learns new tricks more quickly when the ego is not bruised.

The voice-over is an extension of these various forms of natural expression. Voice-over training gives you the skills to draw on your natural expression and to bring a piece of copy to life in a way that serves both the creative team who has written it and the intended audience.

No one is born with voice-over skills, but here are some simple questions you can ask yourself to see if you are suited to voice-over work.

• Do you enjoy being the center of attention?
• Do you like to entertain others?
• Are you compelled to educate and inform?
• Do you need to be heard?

If the answer is yes to all of the above, ask yourself some more specific questions:

- Do those around you describe your voice as warm, sexy, unique, or funny?
- Do you have the natural ability to communicate effectively?
- Do you have the innate ability to modulate voices, create a character, or mimic other voices?

These are terrific talents, gifts that can often be used as supplemental tools to enhance a reading. But the true skill that a voice-over artist needs to master is the ability to take any text, break it down to understand its meaning, and interpret it while staying true to the copywriter's intention. It's a skill that requires time, an open mind, and a good coach to help you learn.

Voice-over artist Keri Tombazian sums up the qualities of a true professional:

> Styles and trends in marketing come and go. A "good" voice will get you a few bookings. A critical ear, technical expertise, and the ability to serve the director will give you a long-lasting career. Don't make it about "how do I sound," make it about "what am I saying?" Animate the words to their meaning. We all grew up learning the music of the English language. The trick is to use that music as naturally and authentically in acting as when speaking first person in our own lives.

WORKING WITH A COACH

Like any performing art, voice-over requires an audience, specifically someone with an objective set of ears who can listen, interpret, and offer constructive criticism. As Lisa Marber-Rich of the Atlas Talent Agency puts it, "Everybody needs coaching."

Finding a coach who works well with you is paramount. You should look for two important qualities in a coach. The first is encouragement: Your coach should be encouraging and allow you the freedom to fail—the best way to learn anything in life is through trial and error. Making mistakes is essential to growth, and shortcomings reveal weaknesses that can assist your coach in pinpointing habits that can be limitations. Bad habits and misguided, preconceived notions can easily be replaced with solid voice-over technique, which, in turn, can become one's strength. That is the glaring difference between a professional voice-over artist and an amateur with a good voice.

The second quality is patience: A coach needs to be patient enough to allow each student to work at his or her own level. It is exciting and rewarding for a teacher or coach to find the true essence of what makes each individual unique and special. A coach who degrades or embarrasses you has no business being a coach. We always find that we have the most success in getting the best perfor- mance from our students when we can pinpoint something positive to say to them before offering notes or a constructive criticism. Our students never feel they don't belong in the booth. We have become convinced that the human psyche learns new tricks more quickly when the ego is not bruised. This universal truth transcends coaching in all its forms, whether on a baseball diamond, on a stage, or in a voice-over booth.

GROUP CLASSES

A voice-over class works on the assumption that everyone learns at the same pace, but, of course, this is rarely the case. Many schools offer a predetermined number of classes as part of a package deal that includes a demo tape. Beware of such classes, as fixed curricula make bold assumptions that newcomers will be ready to compete with the Big Boys in six weeks. Such an assumption can be a recipe for disaster.

A six- to eight-week group voice-over class lacks the personal, one-on-one attention a student needs to thoroughly grasp voice-over skills. In our experience teaching group classes, we have found that it is also necessary, regardless of a student's innate talent, to work one-on-one to refine skills he or she has learned in a group setting.

That said, group workshops and classes offer beginners, interme- diate, and advanced voice-over artists a place to refine basic skills.

Classes offer students a weekly or biweekly opportunity to work out and maintain their voice-over muscles. A group class can be a good place to learn fundamentals, based on the idea that when your classmate is working on a script in the booth you have the opportunity to watch, listen, and learn as an objective observer. It's easier to observe traits in others than in yourself; once you've seen someone else in action and heard what they do right and wrong, you can incorporate these notes into your own work.

CHOOSING A VOICE COACH OR CLASS

Just because a voice-over school or coach places a full-page ad in a well-respected trade publication doesn't mean these instructors have the ability to help launch your career. There are far too many self-proclaimed voice-over coaches who make a nice living luring inexperienced talent but not delivering useful instruction. Word of mouth has always been the best way to get reliable information on who is a good teacher and who is not. People talk, and our business is certainly no exception.

Do your research, and don't make any quick decisions on choosing your coach or class. Be wary of those who take you on as a client without first assessing your talent. A coach should always ask a potential client questions such as,

- "Have you ever worked in voice-overs?"
- "If so, what kind of voice-over work did you do, and where?"
- "Have you had any formal voice-over coaching or acting training in the past?"
- "What are your short-term and long-term goals?"

A well-planned initial dialogue can help a coach determine if you are a student who is ready and eager to learn, not just another wannabe with a lofty dream and a checkbook.

Always ask prospective coaches to play a few of their clients' demo reels. Your own instincts will tell you whether the reels sound professional. It is also a good idea to get some names, phone numbers, and e-mail addresses of former clients. Most voice-over artists are willing

Exercise
Step Right Up to the Microphone

You can practice your voice-over skills any time you record an outgoing message on your answering machine or voice-mail system. The mouthpiece of your telephone or the microphone on your answering machine takes in your words and processes them to the person on the other end of the line. If you record your outgoing message via your phone set, try to determine which of your phones has the best sound. Inexpensive phones tend to not sound as good as the name brands that cost a little more. Once you decide which phone you will use, treat the mouthpiece of your phone just as you would a microphone.

A microphone is an ear. It hears everything you say and can detect every nuance of your voiceprint. How closely you work a microphone will always depend on the type you're using. The pickup pattern of each microphone is different, and you will want to tailor the distance between you and the microphone as well as the direction you speak into it accordingly. Some microphones work better if you speak across them at an angle. With others, you can speak into them straight on. Some sound better when they are at least few inches from your mouth. As a general rule of thumb, make a closed fist, touch the outside of your fist to the mic, and align your mouth to the inside of your fist.

Another "sure shot" tip for when you are using strong air-producing consonants, or plosives, like the letters p, b, or t. Turn your lips away from

---

to share this information without hesitation, as they know that a good voice-over coach or producer can make or break a career.

When you are researching your class options, be sure you will be working in a fully equipped recording studio. You need to train in a soundproof environment and record your voice on a microphone that is specifically engineered to record the spoken word. The more you train in a real-life studio, the more comfortable you will be when you audition or when you are hired to record your voice professionally. When researching a class or a coach, it is a good idea to see

the mic when you vocalize the plosive part of the word, and then turn back and continue speaking. Professional voice-over artists do that little turn trick so quickly that you would never notice. But had they not, you (or the engineer) probably would have heard a giant popping sound. This is true even when leaving a voice message for someone. Treat the mouthpiece of the phone like a microphone and watch those popping *p*'s, *b*'s, and *t*'s!

Listen to your outgoing message as if you are a prospective boss or client, and try to be objective about their perception of you based only on hearing your message. What impression do you think they get from hearing twenty seconds of your voice? Do you come across as charismatic, confident, dependable, depressed, funny, inviting, needy, terse, unfriendly, warm, or any of a long list of other qualities?

If you would like only powerful and positive adjectives to apply to you, make sure your message did not include any missteps.

Does your message sound inviting? Do you wonder why you get more calls than messages? Did you smile as you were recording it? When your face is smiling, the words you say sound happier and more inviting.

On your company voice mail, where you are told to say only your name, does it come across as flat and monotone? Try using a bit more energy in saying your name and lilt it up at the end. Silently ask yourself, Who is the best person I know? Then state your name (aloud) as the answer. Listen to see if it sounds better than the one you recorded before trying this exercise.

---

firsthand where you will be training. You wouldn't enroll in a college or university without first visiting the campus to make sure you would feel comfortable learning there. The environment is important to your studies because, when doing voice-overs, your surroundings are unlike any other you experience in your day-to-day life. You will be in a completely soundproofed enclosure: no echoes, no reverberations, just sonically deadened air, plus headphones and a high-powered microphone that amplifies every rustle of your clothing or intake of breath.

These factors alone can be disconcerting. Imagine what you are likely to feel when you're actually speaking aloud into that microphone, and then imagine going out on job interviews in these conditions. It is vital to train with the proper equipment.

Your class should also provide you with recordings of all your sessions in the booth, along with your coach's comments and feedback. This gives you the opportunity to continue to learn in the comfort of your home.

The bottom line: Do diligent research before you choose your coach or class, and don't make any quick decisions.

Commercials

2

- How to approach a piece of commercial copy
- How to break commercial copy down into sections
- Interpreting the copywriter's intentions
- Making bold and interesting choices for your presentation
- Radio commercials
- Television commercials
- Multiple-person reads

We pretty much take commercials for granted—let's face it, they are an inescapable part of our culture and everyday lives. From the moment we wake to the moment we sleep, we are bombarded with advertisements. Commercials are also part of the career of the majority of people working in voice-overs. Most voice-over work is in commercials, and commercial residuals (monies paid for writing, voicing a character, or appearing in a commercial) are lucrative and a major source of income for a huge workforce of actors, voice artists, singers, musicians, and writers. Without commercials, many of the most talented and creative minds and performers in the arts would lack a reliable source of income. These days, whatever your gender or the regional or ethnic inflection of your voice, you can find work as a voice artist in commercials.

Radio and television commercials differ significantly. As a voice artist you need to be informed well in advance of the medium you are reading for, because it will dictate the approach you will take. In the sections that follow, we'll look at the specifics of how a voice actor should address radio and television copy, but first, let's go over some general approaches to any script that is presented to you.

BRINGING A SCRIPT TO LIFE

Voice artists sometimes take commercial scripts for granted, assuming there is only one intention: to sell a product. It's true that the copywriter's overall, big-picture intention is to generate sales for a product or service, but the art of selling can involve delving much deeper into the human psyche than simply speaking words on a page with gusto. There are no accidents here. Copywriters and creative directors can spend weeks writing and rewriting a single thirty-second radio spot. The copy travels through the creative, account services, and legal departments at the ad agency and is carefully reviewed by the product's client, brand manager, advertising and marketing departments, and sometimes even the company CEO, with numerous revisions along the way. Only then, after everyone on the agency and client sides has signed off on the script, does the spot make its way to the casting director's office and then into the hands of the voice-over artist, who completes this jigsaw puzzle.

The commercial voice artist's job is not simply to read words on the page with the proper diction. Instead, you must analyze, comprehend, and interpret the text so that the written words come alive when spoken—with enough spontaneity, sincerity, and confidence to inspire trust in your listeners. In the end, it's your talent that the ad agencies hope will help convert listeners into paying customers.

How to Analyze Voice-Over Copy

When first approaching copy, read it—that is, just read it, don't speak it—for the sake of understanding the content. On the second silent read-through, read it in your mind as if you were reading a book or newspaper article. Fight the temptation to jump ahead of yourself and perform the script out loud before fully comprehending its purpose.

Determine Your Audience

The next step is to ask yourself (or the person who is conducting the audition, if necessary) who the target audience for this commercial is. Specifically, try to determine the audience's

- Gender
- Age range (ten-year span)

- Economic status
- Cultural environment (urban, suburban, or rural)
- Predicament (problems or issues that need to be solved).

These are the typical elements that help evaluate demographics, the science of population statistics and characteristics that are used especially to identify markets.

Once you have identified the target audience and the predicament, select an individual in your own life to speak to as you read. For example, if the target audience is identified as "male, fifty-five to sixty-five years old, economically burdened, and on the verge of retirement," think of your father, your brother, an uncle, or someone else you know who closely fits that description. There doesn't have to be a perfect parallel between the target audience and your chosen listener, but you will sound far more plausible if you converse with a friend or relative rather than with an imaginary sea of people.

> Even though bold choices are unspoken, they have a profound effect on what is spoken by you, the voice actor.

Remember that most of us don't respond well when we feel we are the target of a sales pitch, so if you personalize the individual you're speaking to, your listeners will not feel quite so "pitched-to." Telemarketers who subscribe to this theory are few and far between. Most blatantly read from scripts and quickly find themselves on the other end of a dial tone.

Making Bold Choices

You will discover clues in your script that will guide you in making what we call bold choices. As an actor, you should always strive to make bold choices, for they allow you to raise the stakes, and they are always far more interesting to act upon than safe choices. You will be perhaps amazed and, we're sure, delighted to discover that even though bold choices are unspoken, they have a profound effect on what is spoken by you, the voice actor.

The actor who fears being wrong makes safe choices. Safe choices can be bland, and more often than not such a read will quickly be forgotten or overlooked. It is the actor who goes out on a limb and is not afraid to make bold choices who typically books the jobs. Casting directors and producers appreciate working with talent who give them an opportunity to scale back a performance as needed. It is always an easier task to tell an actor to back off from a bold choice than to create a more interesting read from a safe choice.

A Silent Read

When you have selected a listener, practice the read again. This time, mouth the words without vocalization (no sound), paying close attention to how you are using your lips, teeth, and tongue. This exercises the muscles in your face, neck, and mouth and begins to create "muscle memory"—that is, your brain begins to recognize the shape and form of the script. Each and every time you read the script, it will become more and more familiar to you, and you will become accustomed to the script physically as well. This repetition greatly reduces the chance of making slip-ups during the audition.

Vocalize the Read

Now that you have read the script in your mind and in your mouth, it is time to vocalize. Increase your voice level by increments, starting with a quiet whisper and moving to a normal speaking level. Read into a portable digital recorder and play your reads back. Playback will allow you to monitor your vocal quality, to recognize the choices you are making as an actor, and to determine whether your performance is close to the instincts you felt when you initially read the spot.

THE RADIO COMMERCIAL

At any given moment, the largest segment of the radio listening audience is traveling in a car. Most radio listeners are commuters, and this audience wants to hear traffic updates, news and weather reports, talk shows, and, of course, music to make the drive more enjoyable. The last thing the radio audience wants to do is listen to commercials. But someone has to pay for "free" radio and the services it provides its audience, and that's why commercials are essential parts of the radio experience.

Radio spots are often entertaining, amusing, and, in some cases, laugh-out-loud funny, even though they are written with a serious purpose in mind: to keep the audience engaged. There is a difference between hearing something and listening to something. Advertisers want you to listen. When you listen you comprehend the messages and grasp the concepts. The human brain has an uncanny ability to recall almost anything as long as there is a purpose attached. In terms of a radio commercial, this means listeners are most likely to remember a message that has meaning and that will directly affect their lives.

Many radio spots require fast talking because they are formatted to fit sixty-second and thirty-second time slots. You can't fit a whole lot of text in that amount of time. However, the human brain can process information at a furious pace, and that's why many spots are read extremely quickly. And when the voice artist is articulate and easy to understand, the audience stays with the message every step of the way.

Let's take a look at a script, a sixty-second radio spot for a hotel chain. Here is the copy, presented as it is printed on the page:

Hotel
60-Second Radio Spot

Well, it's Friday night. You could go to happy hour and hear how unhappy everyone is with their job, their boss, their dinosaur of a computer.

Or you can go to the video store and follow that guy around who's got the last copy of the only movie you want to see, willing him to "put down the tape and step away from the new releases shelf." (He won't.)

Or you could check into the Sunshine with your better half, who you hardly ever see, order room service or watch an in-room movie. Over at the Sunshine Hotel they're giving you 10 to 20 percent off their low weekend rate when you stay two nights, including Friday. It's their new Can't Beat Friday rate.

Just call your travel agent or your local Sunshine Hotel and turn your really long week . . . into a really long weekend. Sunshine. When you're comfortable, you can do anything.

In this spot, the target listener is in a relationship and the copywriter used the term "better half," which implies a female partner. So we deduce that the intended audience is primarily male. Keep in mind that men and women take very different approaches to decision making, especially when it comes to buying products. Men usually buy more impulsively than women, who are more thoughtful and discriminating with their purchasing power.

There are other clues that suggest the audience is male. For instance, a close look at the script reveals that all the activities for this particular Friday night revolve around the hotel room and the activities that take place there: "Order room service" and "watch an in-room movie" may be subtle references to sex. As we all know, sex sells. More important, our target audience of men twenty-five to thirty-five years of age is typically consumed with this desire.

In this instance, the person you will be reading to will be a man in a relationship whose interest is relaxation and romance. If you were to make a bold choice in this case, you would admit (though only internally) that the audience's main objective is time alone with a wife or girlfriend. You do not want to communicate that objective overtly, but the power of that goal should inform your read.

> Playback will allow you to monitor your vocal quality, to recognize the choices you are making as an actor, and to determine whether your performance is close to the instincts you felt when you initially read the spot.

There is an additional appeal: the prospect of saving money and having a great time in the bargain. Notice also that the two references early in the script to discounted entertainment (happy hour and video rental) are consistent with the needs and desires of upwardly mobile men in the twenty-five to thirty-five age range. An analysis of the script's purpose in terms of generating revenue for the client provides a deeper understanding on which to build confidence in delivering the copy in the best possible way for the task at hand.

THE TELEVISION COMMERCIAL

Now let's take a look at an example of a television commercial. This spot is for an insurance company. When you are voicing a television spot, the visuals will always speak for themselves and be the obvious focal point. The voice and the message the voice conveys are supportive, similar to the use of music to enhance the mood and atmosphere in any visual medium, be it a movie, television show, or commercial. Since you are a supporting player, your performance should never steal the focus from the visuals.

Insurance Company
60-Second TV Spot

You will wake up one morning, and there will be no subways
There will be no timesheets or corporate ladders to climb
And in that moment, life will change from a thing to be conquered to a time to be savored
If retirement is a bridge that we must cross when we get there, then we must accept whatever lies in store for us
If it is one we must build . . . then let us begin . . .
Benjamin Franklin . . . Insurance . . . for the unexpected.

The first observation to make is how the spot is laid out on the page. In many cases, the copywriter implies a certain cadence or tone through ellipses, line breaks, and punctuation (or lack thereof). In this case, the copywriter has written in a style that is more "poetic" than prosaic. This should inform the pacing of your read. The delineation of each separate line of this spot implies you should approach your take and read with gravity and a feeling that this content is important.

Note that there is significantly less copy than the allotted time frame of sixty seconds could accommodate. Don't let this confuse you. A television commercial will always supply the imagery during and between the spoken text. Therefore, when the voice artist is not being heard, the spot continues to tell its story. The opposite is true for a radio spot, which lacks visuals that might fill in any "dead" air.

As you would with a radio spot, identify your target audience and then narrow it down to an individual who represents that audience. Analyze the script with some specific questions in mind.

- Are you speaking to a man or a woman?
- How old is this person?
- What is his or her economic situation and cultural environment?
- What predicament or issue he or she is experiencing?

We can deduce that we are speaking, again, to a male audience (note that advertising does not live by politically correct rules; it simply targets the majority to whom the advertiser is marketing). Statistics tell us that men are the primary breadwinners for their families. We can also infer that the targeted men are nearing retirement and therefore are in their mid to late fifties. Economically, these men are in the unpredictable stage in their lives when their regular incomes will soon come to an end. They need to prepare for their futures, because, again as statistics tell us, men are living longer, well into their retirement years. They will need to be financially secure for the remainder of their lives. The ad plays up the uncertainty that most men experience when they approach retirement. It also suggests that retirement is a second life, a time to be savored, so why not enjoy it without financial uncertainty?

Now that you have a more specific notion of the audience, again pick an individual who represents this larger demographic. It might be your father, an uncle, or a close family friend. Since finances can be a sensitive topic, speaking with your subject in a more private locale creates the warmth and intimacy that should come through in your read. Get closer to the microphone and lower the volume of your voice to help achieve the intimacy and honesty required for this delicate conversation. Do not "announce" the script "at" the audience, but rather "talk with" the individual.

The desired effect will be enhanced with the visuals onscreen. In some instances, at your auditions the casting director or the ad agency will provide you with an animated storyboard so that you can see the visual storyline. This, of course, will help you determine the choices and tones you will take in your read. But do not rely on this as a crutch as, in most instances, you will have to rely on your imagination. This opportunity for creativity is what gives voice-over its artistry and cachet.

MULTIPLE-PERSON READS

Multiple-character commercials are written solely for radio. It would be far too confusing and ambiguous if a television spot were to feature more than one announcer. Most multi-character spots are written with comedic flair, another tactic designed to keep the audience engaged long enough to fully understand the product or service that is being advertised. Plus, the characters are often engaged in exaggerated and over-the-top situations.

Such spots require the voice artists to respond and react quickly off one another, keeping the banter alive and moving. Many are written in a sixty-second format and some in less. For a two-person read to work, actors must react quickly so that there is no dead air time between lines from the multiple characters. Dead air time on the radio can be off-putting to the listener. Just as with single-voice reads, the audience is always two steps ahead of you.

A good way to keep the dialogue flowing at a good pace is to read the other character's part while reading your own, so that you do not, for lack of a better term, miss a beat. Always keep your eyes glued to the copy and resist the temptation to engage eye contact with your scene partner; that would only make reading the copy that much more difficult. It will also draw your partner away from his or her own copy and will slow down the pace of the overall read. Think of it as "ear contact," not eye contact. This is a good exercise for all actors, a way to make sure that you are really listening to what the other person has to say.

All good scenes provide characters with a set of intentions. Many of those needs and wants are compromised by the other characters' opposing intentions, creating conflict, which in turn creates drama. In the light-and-fluffy scenarios offered in radio advertising, this conflict often equals comedy. Comedy works when it is grounded in reality. No matter how outlandish a spot may be, a character must still stay true to his or her intentions, thus making the given scenario even funnier. Remember, too, that however funny a scenario is, the goal is always to serve the overall purpose of the advertisement, which is to engage and instruct the audience and convince the audience to take action.

Promos

3

- The business of promos
- Trends in promos
- Types of promos
- Promos for networks and for cable news
- How to find the right promo voice
- Women in promos
- How to succeed in promos
- Exercises: Keep the Fire in Your Belly and Keep It Intense yet Intimate

Promos and image campaigns are sales tools that radio and television networks and local stations design and produce to sell their programs and to remind viewers of the network or station to which they've tuned in. The group of players who do promo work is small but growing. Those who are successful in this part of the industry generally have a good set of pipes, know how to nail the promo in the first or second take, and have the ability to market themselves with a high degree of professionalism, warmth, sincerity, and humor.

THE BUSINESS OF PROMO

Voice-over artists who do promos must have the almost innate ability to do exactly what is required under difficult circumstances. Not only do they read the lines exactly the way the writer envisions them to be read, but they must also know how to shave half a second off that read, if requested. The maximum length of a TV network promo is usually thirty seconds, and that includes excerpts of the show being promoted. Plus, the announcer's voice must be placed so that it does not impede upon any of the sound on tape or sound effects. That's why timing is so important.

Additionally, you must have the ability to instantly voice and deliver whatever clients need whenever they need it. You must also be willing to work as early or late as the show producers or networks work. Let's say you're the promo voice of *American Idol.* Someone is eliminated every week, and new promos must be created for the following week—as soon as one week's episode ends, promos for the following week's show begin immediately. The announcer must be available to voice the promo the moment it is ready. *Entertainment Tonight* and *The Insider* are the most watched daily entertainment news programs in the world. Randy works with both programs, and because breaking celebrity news can happen at any moment, she must be available almost twenty-four hours a day.

If you believe that your niche in the vast world of voice-over is to do promo work and you are not living in a major market (New York, Los Angeles, or Chicago), you should consider how many opportunities there are to do affiliate promo work versus network promo work. There are only a handful of networks, but every city in the country has at least two, three, or four local news channels—and each local news channel employs at least one male and increasingly one female voice to present the station's news promos. Every city in the United States has anywhere from ten, twenty, up to fifty radio stations, with Los Angeles and New York each having more than seventy radio stations.

> "Give 'em what they want until you get in the door, then show 'em what else you got."
>
> —industry saying

Remember, too, that many voice-over artists work remotely. Sometimes producers in the larger markets connect to talent via ISDN (Integrated Digital Services Network), which is why many of today's imaging voices for television networks and affiliates, as well as radio stations, work from homes all across America. These select voice talents rise every day to face their microphone, armed with a diverse assemblage of copy that demands a very quick turnaround.

Randy lives on the Gulf coast of Florida. Her daily work with *Entertainment Tonight* and *The Insider* begins as early as 5:00 A.M. Pacific Time. Luckily for Randy, that's 8:00 A.M. Eastern Time! When you work with the networks, you're a team player, so long days can be part of the work. It's like having "golden handcuffs": Even if you had the key, you wouldn't use it.

Brian Lee, voice-over artist for all the major networks, as well as for movie trailers and, television affiliates, lives in the same locale and is frequently needed by West Coast producers late into the evening. He has tracked as late as 2:00 A.M.. Joe Cipriano, the voice of NBC dramas and specials as well as numerous Fox comedy promos, including *The Simpsons,* lives in Los Angeles and is often called as early as 6:00 A.M. to track with New York. That means not only waking early but being in full voice when you're needed and keeping it going all day long.

TRENDS IN PROMO

The types of voices that are sought after for promos change all the time. Let's look at how the voices in promo have changed over the years.

Brian Lee has this to say about a phenomenon named Don LaFontaine, one of the most famous voices in promos today:

> There is a man in our industry who is our god, our Founding Father . . . The 'Don.' 'In a world' . . . I believe Don coined that unforgettable phrase. Because of Don's career in trailers, we can all thank him for the very structure of movie trailer and network television promo production today. A promo line, then a sound bite, followed by another promo line, et cetera.

Don's voice is so recognizable that the creators of the Geico Insurance commercials used him in their campaign with the knowledge that viewers across America would know exactly who he was once they heard his voice. Don's trademark voice created the paradigm for many of today's successful announcers. His voice style is one of those that, at least every decade or so, hits its mark and creates a shift in demographics skewing to the younger audience that the networks continue to vie for.

The people who choose the voices for promos, usually marketing directors, tend to go with a known entity. That is true in the talent they select as well as the style of read that identifies a network. Currently, there is a trend toward a deep, resonant tone for networks as well as drama and reality shows, and over the past several decades, voice style has shifted from the parental voice to the peer-influenced voice that informs rather than demands.

Promo style is ever-changing. "If you were doing promo ten years ago," says Brian Lee, "you're doing it differently now. It just changes, and you've got to stay with the style and the times when you read promos."

The promo read also varies according to which network you are working for. At the website www.voicebank.net, you can listen to voice-over artists who specialize in promo. You will hear the types of voices and voice styles that network, cable channel, and local affiliates are utilizing these days. Be sure to listen carefully. These are working voice actors who have successfully marketed their style to their buyers.

Once you have a basic understanding of how the promo voice underscores the message in the promo announcement for a given message, you can have fun challenging your acting and voice range. The saying goes, "Give 'em what they want until you get in the door, then show 'em what else you've got." Who knows? Perhaps your particular sound delivery will be exactly what the network and cable channels are looking for in the coming years.

TYPES OF PROMOS

The promo read is specific to the demographic, programming, and content of the channel. On top of this, there are a particular sound and methodology to promos that seem to remain popular and consistent over the years. Here are some examples of promo copy. In all promos, the announcer reads only the text printed in upper-case type. The other lines are those of the talking heads featured in the promo. We call such non-voice-over lines SOTs (sounds on tape); they can be dialogue, music, sound effects, or any combination of the three. The promo announcer's job is to set up each clip with maximum appeal and impact.

The Voice of the Promo Read Today

The unique aspect of the promo read is that each line is left hanging in anticipation of the sound bite from the show or SOT (sound on tape), and not vocalized in a nailed-down or definitive manner. This lets the viewers know that there is something coming right up that they should pay attention to! It is only at the end of the promo message, when the announcer tags it out (finishes the promotional message) with the time and network name, that we are meant to feel that the spot has come to a conclusion.

Years ago, there was a traditional "announcer voice" that gave us this information. Today it is the "non-announcer" type read that works. The voice tends to have a very conversational style that was made popular first by MTV, VH-1, and other youth-oriented networks.

In-Show Promo

An "in-show" promo runs within a show and teases a future story, perhaps airing on a different day. Here's an example:

TINA FEY FROM THIRTY ROCK!

POSES AS BRITNEY!

JENNA FISCHER FROM THE OFFICE!

DOES LINDSAY LOHAN!

AND SARAH SILVERMAN!

TEASES YOU AS AMY WINEHOUSE!

SOT: I know I look amazing.

INSIDE THE NEW VANITY FAIR LADIES OF

LAUGHTER ISSUE!

AND FIND OUT WHAT POP ICONS SANDRA BERNHARD,

AMY SEDARIS, SUSIE ESSMAN, AMY POEHLER, AND WANDA SYKES

ARE PLAYING!!!

SOT: I never thought I'd be in *Vanity Fair*. I thought I'd have to maybe kill Oprah and that would be the story—literally kill Oprah.

ET'S BEHIND THE SCENES WITH THE AMAZING ANNIE LEIBOVITZ!

Sound effects and visuals:

CLICK CLICK CLICK—GODDESS SHOTS

SOT: My mind is blown now.

MONDAY!!

The "Daily" Promo

This type of promo "teases" a show that will run later that day. These promos are updated every day, teasing that day's show. For instance, every station that airs *The Insider* airs a daily promo teasing that day's show content.

Daily Promo for The Insider

NEXT INSIDER!

QUEEN ELIZABETH!!!

AT HOME AND UNGUARDED!!!

MORE FROM THE BARBARA WALTERS EXCLUSIVE!

SOT: Barbara got glimpses of the royal family like you've never seen before.

INSIDE THE SECRET LIVES OF WILLIAM! HARRY! AND PRINCE CHARLES!

THEN KATIE! KATHERINE!

WE COUNT DOWN THE TOP TEN CELEBRITY WEDDING DRESSES OF ALL TIME!

NEXT INSIDER!

Television Affiliate News Promo

The competition between local stations to earn the viewer's trust is fierce. The intent of most news promos is to get you to tune into the next newscast in search of the life-saving or life-enhancing information that supposedly only this channel can provide. Each news channel touts its commitment to being better and faster at giving you the most up-to-date information about anything and everything that can affect your world. So it makes sense that the voices behind these promos must be as strong, warm, reliable, emphatic, and dependable as the stations they represent. The job of the announcer is to compel viewers

to watch only this news channel—for stories and information they can't get anywhere else. In 2008, Randy replaced the male voice that New York's My9 WWOR TV had used for years, and here's a promo she did for the station:

WHO SAYS YOU NEED TO BE THIN TO HAVE A HEALTHY BODY?

Fitness Girl SOT: I have clients who are overweight who run marathons.

A FEW EXTRA POUNDS DOESN'T MEAN GETTING FIT IS OUT OF REACH.

Woman SOT: You kind of look at yourself and say . . . am I really the one who's able to exercise like this?

EASY WAYS TO HAVE A HEALTHY BODY WHILE CARRYING A FEW EXTRA POUNDS . . .

TONIGHT ON MY9 NEWS AT TEN,

AFTER PARADISE HOTEL 2.

Television Sports Affiliate Promo

Again, the job of the announcer is to compel viewers to watch only this particular sports channel. Here is a spot for a Fox Sports Network affiliate called FSN Live.

FSN LIVE IS YOUR ALL-ACCESS PASS TO THE ACTION YOU LIVE FOR AND THE TEAMS YOU CAN'T LIVE WITHOUT . . .

FSN LIVE CONNECTS YOU TO THE PLAYERS AND EVENTS LIKE NO ONE ELSE CAN . . .

WITH CAMERAS ON NORTHWEST UNIVERSITIES, AND IN-DEPTH COVERAGE FROM OUR EXPERT ANALYSTS WARREN MOON, BILL KRUEGER, AND CRAIG EHLO . . .

EXPERIENCE THE NORTHWEST SPORTS SCENE LIKE NEVER BEFORE . . .

FSN LIVE . . . WHERE THE ACTION IS . . .

BEFORE THE GAME, AFTER THE GAME, AND EVERY NIGHT AT 10.

This piece of copy was written to persuade football fans in the Pacific Northwest to tune in to FSN Live. It promises to provide more in-depth coverage of the viewer's favorite regional teams than any other station will. Sometimes the same copy is used for both TV and radio. Studies show that television viewers and radio listeners are often multitasking, so an audio cue is necessary to get the audience to actually look at the TV or listen to the radio. That's why this text should be read with a lot of energy in order to tap into viewers' and listeners' sports enthusiasm. Bringing this copy to life requires an attitude of ownership, as though you are the biggest football fan on the planet and you know that no other channel can give you all the behind-the-scenes dirt, both before and after the game.

It might seem that this copy should be read by a booming male voice in order to appeal to macho male football fans. However, this particular piece of copy was ultimately recorded by a female voice. The producers at FSN Live wanted to use a female voice to appeal to their male football fans and to include their female viewers as well.

"Topical" News Promotional Announcement

Topicals are daily news teases, and reading them is among the most time-sensitive work in our industry. They concern daily stories that change and are almost never repeated. They are time-critical in a couple of ways.

First, each line within the script must be delivered with the exact timing specified by the writer. Most promos air in thirty-, twenty-, fifteen-, ten-, or even five-second lengths. The announcer only has a certain amount of time to deliver a line, and timing is even more critical if a sound bite is going to be added into the promo. The writers will generally include the length of the sound bite(s), so the announcer must do the math and figure out how much time he or she has to deliver the lines.

Second, promos must be returned to the segment producer as quickly as possible so the station can match the voice-over to picture and get the segment on air just before an upcoming newscast. When producing a news promo, the producer/editor places the announcer's voice in the videotaped segments to create a news promo.

Notice how the following read differs from a commercial in that you're not trying to sell a product or service. Instead, you're enticing the viewer/listener to tune into the full story ("An Exercise-less Diet") at a specific date and time ("Tonight at 6") after hearing only a snippet ("She lost 150 pounds in just nine months with no exercise"). Promos are all about the tease.

:30

SOT: If someone hasn't seen me in a long time, they just can't believe it.

SHE LOST 150 POUNDS IN JUST NINE MONTHS WITH NO EXERCISE . . .

SOT: I woke up that morning, looked in the mirror, and said that was it.

WHY THE SECRET TO HER DIET IS EATING EVERYTHING—*IN REVERSE.*

SOT: Old, young, children, adults, men women? Anyone can do this plan.

SOT: If I could do it, anyone could do it.

A SPECIAL FOR YOUR HEALTH. TONIGHT AT SIX ON WYFF NEWS FOUR. LIVE LOCAL BREAKING NEWS.

TUESDAY AT SIX ON WYFF NEWS FOUR. LIVE LOCAL BREAKING NEWS.

Television Affiliate News Image Spot

This spot for a television affiliate would run throughout a news image campaign. These are generally created during sweeps ratings periods—the months of September, November, February, and May. This spot is selling an early morning show, and in this case the local news channel is pointing out the fact that its show is tied to the CBS network's *Morning Show.* So, you're selling not only your channel but also the fact that only your channel is a CBS affiliate. The ultimate point is, of course, to get listeners to tune into News Channel 32.

<VERSION 1; +/- :25>

BEFORE YOU START YOUR 9 TO 5,

SPEND 5 TO 9 WITH NEWS CHANNEL 32 . . .

AND THE EARLY SHOW.

WITH ABBY MILLER.

PAUL MOSES.

KIM STEVENS.

HARRY SMITH.

HANNAH STORM.

JULIE CHEN.

RENE SYLER.

AND DAVE PRICE.

WAKE UP TO NEWS CHANNEL 32 IN THE MORNING, AND THE EARLY SHOW.

WORKING HARD FOR YOU FROM 5 TO 9 . . .

BEFORE YOU START YOUR 9 TO 5.

<VERSION 2; +/- :25>

BEFORE YOU GO TO WORK,

LET NEWS CHANNEL 32 WORK FOR YOU.

NEWS CHANNEL 32 IN THE MORNING . . .

AND THE EARLY SHOW.

GET THE LATEST NEWS, ENTERTAINMENT, HEALTHWATCH, AND WEATHER WITH

NEWS CHANNEL 32 IN THE MORNING, AND THE EARLY SHOW.

WORKING HARD FOR YOU,

BEFORE YOU GO TO WORK.

The read should be authoritative, yet warm enough to convince viewers to start their day with this group of people. Mornings are a friendlier time of day—announcers take a different tone than they would for 6:00 P.M. or 10:00 P.M. news, which would require a more serious and dramatic tone. This early-morning-show promo requires a read that is more in line with a warm and friendly sentiment like "Wake up and start your day with orange juice, coffee, and this channel only!"

Sweeps Piece

Sweeps are periods of time during the year when television networks and their station affiliates have their audiences "measured" demographically to see which networks and stations are most popular. These measurements enable the stations to set the fees they charge advertisers, which are directly connected to a station's profitability. A sweeps piece generally touts the most outrageous stories that a legitimate news channel can offer in order to grab viewers and compel them to watch. This sweeps piece obviously would be shocking, and any parent would have to tune in. The writing, as well as the read, tap into the shock value in this story.

WONDER IF YOUR TEEN IS HAVING SEX?
WONDER HOW YOUNG THEY START?
WONDER WHY THEY DO IT?

TUESDAY AT 6 AND 11 ON WYFF NEWS 4. LIVE, LOCAL, BREAKING NEWS.

TONIGHT AT 6 AND 11 ON WYFF NEWS 4. LIVE, LOCAL, BREAKING NEWS.

TONIGHT AT 11 ON WYFF NEWS 4. LIVE, LOCAL, BREAKING NEWS

This read is urgent, darker, going for shock value. Note here, incidentally, that three separate tags are being recorded: "Tuesday at 6," "Tonight at 6," and "Tonight at 11." The engineer will insert each recorded tag into an appropriate time slot.

Radio Imaging

When you're alone in your car listening to the radio or sitting at your desk, you connect with the disk jockeys (DJs) on your favorite music radio stations. As the voice of a radio station, the job of the DJ is to share information with listeners that reinforces why this is the perfect radio station for them.

97.1 WASH-FM . . . THANKS FOR MAKING US YOUR CHOICE AS WASHINGTON'S HOME FOR THE HOLIDAYS . . . AND WAIT'LL YOU

HEAR WHAT'S COMING NEXT . . . DETAILS DECEMBER 26TH . . . HAPPY HOLIDAYS . . . FROM WASHINGTON'S NUMBER 1 AT WORK STATION . . . 97.1 WASH-FM.

97.1 WASH-FM . . . WASHINGTON'S HOME FOR THE HOLIDAYS ONCE AGAIN THIS YEAR.

AND MAKE SURE TO STICK AROUND AFTER THE HOLIDAYS. DETAILS ON WHAT'S NEXT, DECEMBER 26TH . . . ON WASHINGTON'S NUMBER 1 AT WORK STATION . . . 97.1 WASH-FM.

97.1 WASH-FM . . . THANKING YOU FOR SPENDING YOUR HOLIDAY SEASON WITH OUR FAMILY. MAKE SURE TO KEEP YOUR DIAL SET AT 97.1 AFTER THE HOLIDAYS, TOO. DETAILS DECEMBER 26TH . . . FROM WASHINGTON'S NUMBER 1 AT WORK STATION . . . 97.1 WASH-FM.

MERRY CHRISTMAS . . . FROM OUR FAMILY TO YOURS. WASHINGTON'S NUMBER 1 AT WORK STATION . . . 97.1 WASH-FM.

97.1 WASH-FM . . . HELPING *YOU* STAY WARM, WITH THE WASH-FM VACATION-A-DAY GIVEAWAY. WAKE UP WITH LOO AND LORI ON THE WASH-FM MORNING SHOW FOR DETAILS. A VACATION *EVERY* DAY (BEGINNING MONDAY) . . . FROM WASHINGTON'S NUMBER 1 AT WORK STATION . . . 97.1 WASH-FM.

With this piece of copy, aired during the holiday season, we're targeting the emotions that people feel during this time of year by reminding them how grateful we are as a radio station to have them listening. The read in this case is warm, friendly, and sincere. All the while, we are selling them on the value of continuing to listen to our radio station. In the last piece of copy we hear a tease for the listener to tune in for a trip to somewhere fabulous, so that detail should be read with the excitement of something new being offered.

Cable News

Cable news has changed the TV landscape for announcers. Each channel vies for increased viewership by using particular (and, they hope, "ownable") types of voices detailing why their news channel is the one with the most late-breaking news stories, the most in-depth information, or the most intelligent analyses. Even their particular political slant can be part of their branding process and their selling message.

While CNN tends to give each program its own branding voice, for many years the network employed James Earl Jones to be its corporate umbrella brand-voice. It's no accident that when we heard Jones, we'd know we were watching CNN.

FOX News has created a more highly targeted announcer profile, in an attempt to attract younger viewers by using a younger male voice. The voices we hear are announcers who use a more real sound. The read for that sound is more from the throat than from the abdomen. This type of read gives the promo a youthful yet urgent feeling.

DEVELOPING THE RIGHT READ

When Randy was chosen for the *Entertainment Tonight* and *The Insider* gigs, her life changed for the better. Being the voice of the most-watched entertainment news magazines in the world is a thrill to her.

Finding her read for these programs was a delightful challenge for Randy. Her natural read for promo is generally a darker, no-smile delivery. It can sometimes sound more staccato, emphasizing certain words by inflecting downward, not upward as we do in general conversation. This process of finding a distinct way to bring meaning to copy is called "finding your money read." This is why they want you! Clients believe that you have the ability to take their words, find your money read, and sell their message better than anyone else can.

When you work for certain news and television shows, the expected read has already been established by the writers who pen the promos. It is up to the voice talent to determine where their money read plays into the promo that they're voicing. You have to listen closely to the producers to know exactly which read they want you to deliver—it may require you to go from urgent to caring to shocked or salacious, bringing each word to life.

Your money read is the read the buyers deem is your best read. You can vary your tone and projection to deliver your best promo read. It is the reason you were hired. Someone heard your money read and decided that is the voice they want to sell their show, network, or newscast. It is always a good idea to know exactly what your money read is and how to deliver it on demand.

Randy's money read for *Entertainment Tonight* and *The Insider* is one that spits out the headlines into your ears, the same way a magazine cover grabs your attention in the checkout line. Just as these magazines draw you to reach out and buy them, Randy's read makes you pick up the remote to watch those shows.

Going from urgent, yet heartfelt, to sexy and outrageous is like turning on a dime. You must be able to make the various vocal cues almost instantly without thinking about it. Once this kind of approach to reading copy is engrained, you will be able to market yourself as the one who does it better than the rest.

In 2006, Linda Bell Blue, executive producer of *Entertainment Tonight* and *The Insider,* had a vision as to how these CBS Television Distribution shows could win in the highly competitive sweeps period by featuring Don LaFontaine and Randy as the exclusive voices. Using a male-female combination to sell a daily syndicated show had not been done before the pairing of Randy and Don. The shows are the reigning winners during sweeps due to the combination of voices and production value that are part of the branding for these entertainment news magazines. The director/producer of the two shows, Kevin Gershan, worked with Don and Randy to make Linda's vision a reality. Since January 2008, Randy has run with this ball on her own and is the show's only voice.

FIND THE MUSIC

Promos are highly stylized. They tend to be written in a way that demands a specific rhythm and pace. In fact, there is an iambic pentameter in almost every piece of copy written. Iambic pentameter

Exercise
Keep the Fire in Your Belly

To better understand how the most successful men and women in trailers and promos read copy with passion, drama, and gravitas, try the following exercise. Find a piece of promo copy (copy it from a dramatic show promo on TV or from one of the trailers on a rental DVD) and read the copy with impact. If you are projecting too much your read will sound too loud; during a recording, an overly loud reading would no doubt cause over-modulation (that is, one in which the speaker's voice causes the microphone to distort). Sudden, intense volume drives the listener or viewer away from the source. When done right, promos and trailers draw you closer.

If your initial read was too loud or over-projected, a director would tell you to lessen the projection of air/volume behind your voice. In other words, control the volume at which you are speaking but keep the same amount of fire in your belly. In the movies the villains who deliver death threats not with a yell but in a whisper, who sort of lean in and speak softly so no one else can hear, are the ones who give us the chills.

Delivering a great dramatic promo read is not as difficult a challenge. No one dies in promo. But the promos that really grab you have something about them that creates a sense of urgency and are compelling because you don't want to miss watching that show—and that, of course, is the intent.

---

is a five-beat poetic line, the most common rhythm in poetry. Shakespeare's "The quality of mercy is not strained" is the classic example of iambic pentameter. This is true not only for promo but also for trailers, narration, and sometimes commercial copy. Your job is to find the music in every piece of copy you read. This does not mean that it should sound singsong; it should, however, flow with a cadence that suits the message.

The copywriters at *Entertainment Tonight* and *The Insider* love alliterations, the repetition of initial sounds: "From a Bridal Bouquet Blunder to a Risqué Reception Routine, it's more Weddings Gone

Exercise
Keep It Intense yet Intimate

Here is a scene for you to imagine: You walk into the house and see your husband/wife in an embrace with someone—he or she is clearly cheating on you. The script says you respond with shock and great anger and scream, "What the hell are you doing? How could you?"

Now, let's say you have kids, and you know the children are sleeping just down the hall. A responsible parent would not scream at the top of his or her lungs and would instead speak at a volume that could not be heard more than three to five feet away.

The idea is to deliver the same line with less projection but the same shock and horror. "What the hell are you doing? How could you?" In this case you need to access the same fire in your belly, but you can't scream or over-project. Instead, the goal is to keep it intense yet intimate.

Now, using this tactic, try reading this promo:

TODAY AT 3 ON NBC4 . . . THE BIG APPLE WANTS BIG JUSTICE . . .
AND NOW YOU'RE GETTING IT . . .
THIS NEW JERSEY NURSE SAYS HER EX BORROWED CASH TO PAY BILLS . . .
    SOT: I lent him $1,600
    SOT: I don't know where she gets this figure from.
BUT DID HE BLOW THE MONEY ON DRUGS?
    SOT: You're under the influence right now. I can tell. Look at ya.
AFTER JUDGE JOE LINES UP THE FACTS . . .
    SOT: She actually sent you to rehab.
HE SMELLS SERIOUS TROUBLE . . .
    SOT: You are a sorry pathetic specimen because you want to die.
JUDGE JOE BROWN TAKES ON NEW YORK . . . TODAY AT 3 ONLY ON NBC4!

Wild!" You can see where the music is in this example, just by finding the alliteration.

An advantage to working in the studio is that you have the ability to read to visuals, which give you a clue as to how you should do the read. If you don't know or understand what the producers and writers want you to do, just ask. Producers and writers love to tell you what they had in mind when they wrote a particular spot or created a campaign.

If you are working from your home studio and cannot reach the writer or producer, go ahead and do several takes, explaining that you have three very different reads for them to consider because you were unable to get the necessary feedback before you voiced a particular spot or audition. That way you are showing them how professional you are by considering their needs.

SO, WHERE ARE THE WOMEN?

Why do you tend to hear more men than women in voice-over spots? Women collectively have as many types of voices as are needed to deliver the many different reads in this area of the business. Change takes time, however, and it comes down to the executives who make the marketing decisions. Many still believe that the target demographic of eighteen- to thirty-four-year-old men "don't want to hear a woman tell them what to watch." Even worse, the perception has been that if a woman's voice is selling a show or network it must be a "chick flick" or Lifetime. Only recently have we begun to hear more female voices being integrated with those of men. This is especially true in local television affiliate news promos.

> "The voice artist needs to nail the read on the first take and be competitive with anyone who currently voices trailers and network promos."
>
> —Jonn Wasser, Atlas Talent Agency

It is good to hear a woman tease a news story that is about something other than breast cancer or menopause. As voice-over artist Anne Gartlan puts it, "Women are concerned with nuclear holocaust, too." The other types of channels that utilize female-voiced promos are those dedicated to life, health, children, family, and education. Female announcers can also be heard in abundance on the Style Network, Home & Garden, and other networks that market specifically to women. The read on these channels is an intimate "matter-of-fact" read, kind of like a woman speaking to her best girlfriend. She is simply imparting some very hip information that entices women to tune in and learn about the latest trends in decorating, cooking, makeup, or fashion must-haves.

The soft, breathy female read is still pretty much relegated to soap operas and some sexy reality or game shows. You would expect to hear this voice on the Playboy Channel or other adult-only programming. You even hear men delivering that kind of read for these shows.

SECRETS OF SUCCESS

In chapter 9, we give you a step-by-step breakdown of what a voice talent needs to do to create a winning promo demo. Having the vision of one day becoming a big-time network promo announcer is great motivation for an aspiring talent, but you need to be realistic. To get experience necessary to compete at that level, consider starting as an announcer on a local public broadcast station or a smaller-market television or radio stations, none of which can afford highly experienced talent.

The top ten stations in each market have at least two voices that handle the on-air imaging duties, and they have the most dollars available for the best talent. In order to compete with this talent, according to Jonn Wasser of the Atlas Talent Agency, "the voice artist needs to nail the read on the first take and be competitive with anyone who currently voices trailers and network promos." And yes, there are radio stations as well as Internet radio stations that pay as little as fifty dollars a month for a voice, and you can be sure there are plenty of voice talents lined up for even that small piece of the pie.

In addition to honing your talents, knowing how to get along with your clients and producers when you're not actually reading the copy can be a big plus in a long-lasting business relationship. Voice-over artist Anne Gartlan says she worked with a producer in Baltimore who left and went to Jacksonville and took her with him; then he left and went to Miami and he took her there, too.

It's frequently true that when the producer/writer of a spot arrives in the studio, you get the feeling that you are nothing more than an interruption in his day. (For those of us who work from our home studios, the same idea can apply.) In many cases the producer/writer is in his or her twenties or early thirties and can be a little (or a lot) intimidated by the voice-over talent with whom he is about to work. Being professional by arriving early and doing your work in one or two takes can alleviate a lot of stress from your side of the glass into the studio's control room. Every bit of your "people talent" is useful in stressed studio conditions.

The fact that you are reading this book places you in a unique category of up-and-coming artists who will embrace this knowledge. Your eagerness to learn the tricks of the trade may serve you well in your new or continuing endeavor to make voice-over work your vocation, not just an avocation.

Narration

4

- Broadcast narration
- Why less is more
- *Hooked on Phonics*: A non-broadcast success story
- Telephony and other non-broadcast media
- Voice for Hire: Barry Zate

Tune in to A&E, the Discovery Channel, Animal Planet, the History Channel, Home & Garden, the Food Network, or PBS and you'll stumble upon programming that uses a voice-over narrator. Narration refers to the voice that guides you through television shows such as documentaries, biographies, educational programming, science and nature shows, and even reality shows. Narrators also work in non-broadcast programming such as corporate and instructional-training videos, industrials, trade-show presentations, websites, and audiobooks.

The narrator must serve the intention and vision of the writer and director. In order for the audience to believe and understand the information being presented, the narrator must first understand the copy. With this understanding we can share the information with a delivery that is real, informative, and easy to comprehend. But this doesn't mean you must be a scientist or a doctor in order to understand the writing when doing a narration for the Discovery Channel about the inner workings of the human brain. You simply must be able to impart to the viewer the amazing wonders of the brain (and hope your tongue follows suit). When casting is done for a narration piece, the breakdown (casting specification) usually requests that the narrator be a storyteller, along with any other particulars the client may desire, such as a deep voice or a "regular guy" kind of read. There are more occasions today than there were in the past when clients ask for a woman's interpretation of the story.

BROADCAST NARRATION

Randy was hired to narrate a five-part series called *The Secret History Of. . . .* The challenge was not only to complete each show in a timely manner with only one or two passes at each narration segment but also to give it the distinctive style the producer wanted. Randy had been hired to replace another voice-over artist. The fact that she was the second voice-over talent hired to do this job indicated that the producers were already behind schedule, so a relatively quick understanding of the task at hand was essential.

The subjects on *The Secret History Of . . .* ran the gamut from Harley-Davidson motorcycles to President Clinton to showmen and sideshows to Las Vegas. In order to best capture the intent of the writer, Randy simply let the visuals speak to her and used the narrative to set up each sound-bite, or section, of narration. She was careful to deliver the material without a smile, giving the read a serious, straightforward tone that complemented the job properly and pleased the clients.

For another television documentary that still airs on various cable channels, *UFO's over Phoenix,* Randy met briefly with the film's producer before she stepped into the booth. Viewing segments from the film of UFO sightings and "other-worldly" encounters led her to the artistic choice of a dark, subtle read. She worked in her lower vocal range, barely projecting into the microphone in order to keep the narration dramatic and intriguing. Randy knew her job was to present the facts and not make any judgment about whether these events actually occurred. As a rule, narrators never indicate their own opinions or attitudes toward subjects, but instead strive to embody the vision of the producer or the casting director.

LESS IS MORE IN NARRATION

In 2003, filmmaker John Biffar wrote and directed a documentary called *The Fireboats of 9/11.* The project was created to honor his father, a retired New York City fireboat captain, and to relate the haunting circumstances that brought the old fireboats out of retirement on September 11, 2001. John recorded the temporary voice track (also known as a scratch track) during the video-editing session, and colleagues thought no one would be able to match his passion, knowledge, emotion, and sincerity. The History Channel, however, found John's read too emotional and decided to hire a top male voice-over artist to narrate the show instead. John's experience shows us that sometimes the creator of the story may sometimes be too close to the piece to give an objective read.

When it comes to vocal projection and emotion, sometimes less is more. To make that determination, you need to do the research to know what the network is looking for based on the types of voices they have chosen in the past to do their narrations. Simply watching the various cable channels and listening carefully to the voices you hear on each network can give you a clue. Then bring that particular level of intensity, and emotion, to the piece you are reading for that network or channel.

> It is a confidence-building experience to make the client happy then go a step beyond.

When in doubt about what kind of read to bring to a piece, always do exactly as the producer and/or casting director asks you to do. At the point when you "hit the mark" and they are satisfied, always ask for another take before you move on or the session ends. This is your gift. You now have an opportunity to give the read a little sizzle. This is the take where you can deliver your own special read without the emotional burden of wondering if they are happy with your work, because they have already told you they were satisfied with the previous take. Having nothing to lose allows you, the actor, to take a chance. Sometimes you strike gold, and if you don't, well . . . you know they are happy with the take you have already delivered. It is a confidence-building experience to make the client happy and then go a step beyond. You can sometimes delight and surprise not only the client but also yourself in these moments.

NON-BROADCAST NARRATION

The makers of pharmaceuticals and developers of the latest technology present their latest products and research breakthroughs to their buyers, usually in a film/video format. The retail, real estate, and financial industries also hire voice talent on a regular basis. The trick to narrating industrials is to not only to be able to pronounce words you have never seen or heard before in a knowledgeable and clear manner but to breathe life into text that could otherwise be very dry and technical. Developing this special ability to make industrial copy come alive poses a wonderful challenge. If you have an innate ability to read and pronounce words fluidly and flawlessly by breaking them down phonetically, industrials may be in your future.

Hooked on Phonics: A Non-Broadcast Narration Success Story

In 1986, Randy was asked to be the voice of an exciting new educational program called *Hooked on Phonics,* created by entrepreneur John Shanahan to teach children how to read using the phonetic interpretation of ordinary spelling. Up until this point Randy had been a broadcaster—more specifically, a rock 'n' roll disc jockey—so this opportunity presented a whole new area of interest, work, and income for her, and *Hooked on Phonics* became a phenomenon and a household name.

As a matter of fact, those famous commercials were everywhere in the early 1990s, heard on the radio or television every thirty seconds somewhere in America. To date, more than two million families and thousands of teachers have embraced *Hooked on Phonics* to help them teach their children to read—from the ABCs to high school–level reading comprehension.

It took hundreds of hours to record *Hooked on Phonics,* because the program was created before digital editing became common practice. Randy had to read every lesson four times in a row! It took enormous patience and control to maintain a consistent, helpful, and cheerful performance level throughout such a lengthy recording process, but Randy's concentration paid off. Over the past twenty years, she has updated the program eight times, marking a twenty-two-year relationship of mutual respect and productivity (and employment!). For a voice actor, that's the ultimate gratification.

John Shanahan, creator and former owner of *Hooked on Phonics*, says this about his work with Randy:

> When I first created Hooked on Phonics I had hired a male voice as the instructional voice and was looking for a gal to do the commercials. I used a studio in Orange County where one of the engineers said to me that he knew a young woman who was a DJ on the rock station KMET in Los Angeles. So I had him bring her in to read some commercials I wrote after purchasing that now famous telephone number 1 800-ABC-DEFG!
>
> After hearing Randy read my commercials I was not only sold on Randy Thomas as the perfect spokeswoman for my product, but I knew immediately that I had to scratch everything I had done to that point and record the program again with Randy as my instructional voice. Over the years, I heard time and time again that both parents and children enjoy learning to read by listening to the infectious smile that Randy so naturally infuses into every lesson.

Randy's work with *Hooked on Phonics* led her to an invitation from Dr. Dorothy Taguchi, a doctor of linguistics, to become the voice of her accent reduction program, *Accent America: Pronounce English with an American Accent.* As you, too, will find out, one good thing opens the door to another!

TELEPHONY

Corporate voice greetings are a great way for beginning voice artists to get their feet wet. When you are the first voice someone hears when they call a business, you are responsible for the first impression the caller has about that company. Imagine that you are a cheerleader and the company is the team you are rooting for. Your voice should let callers know that they have just reached a winning team. Be proud, clear, and confident when letting someone know that their call is important and they will be connected as quickly as possible to the person they are calling.

One of Peter's first voice-over jobs was recording a friend's corporate voice greeting for a prominent real estate company. The friend needed an outgoing voice message that sounded both friendly and professional and asked Peter, a trained actor, if he could record the message as well as accompanying prompts. Peter realized quickly that it would be a challenge to record so much material in one fell swoop directly onto the phone system, in much the same way it can be difficult to record a complicated outgoing message onto a home answering machine. The recording took much longer than anticipated and didn't go as smoothly as planned, so Peter and his friend decided to rent a recording studio and digitally record the message and each prompt separately, giving the sound engineer several takes with which to work. The various elements were then converted into a continuous sound file. Peter had a blast recording the material and thought, "I could do this more often and actually get paid for it."

Peter's second telephonic job came from a diamond wholesaler who heard his voice and liked it when he called the real-estate firm. He hired Peter at a rate of $250 an hour, and since then, Peter has voiced greetings and phone prompts for numerous companies of all sizes, and always enjoys doing the work.

The biggest reason Peter feels he's worked so consistently in this genre is the nature of his voice. He's been told his voice is clear and friendly, professional without sounding intimidating or unapproachable. The business world has changed over the years—it's reaching out to a younger, less formal audience, and the vocal styles in voice greetings reflect that.

Voice for Hire: Barry Zate

Barry Zate started out as a disk jockey and later as a radio station production director. He is a cofounder of IMAGE Teleproducts. Barry has worked professionally since he was fourteen years old, often voicing spots and promos. He has worked for ABC, NBC, CBS, Mutual Networks, and Viacom. In addition to his daily work with IMAGE Teleproducts, which creates and records voice messages for companies and other clients, Barry continues to do voice acting for radio, TV, and industrials nationwide.

Professional voice messages for telephones are a huge business. Within the past two years, we have seen a 150 percent growth in our business.

I'm sure you've heard the term "voice jail." If you ask yourself why people consider voice jail (or more accurately, Automated Attendants) a pain, it's usually because the voice drones on with a million choices, and few of them get callers what they want. The most important parts of a voice greeting are clear, concise instructions, and a read that is not too fast and not too slow. Think of the people who are calling in. Some are half listening, or are on speakerphones and cell phones. Some are frustrated and just want to talk with someone. As with any read, you've got to know your audience, understand why they are calling, and deliver your message accordingly. Tempo, clarity, and direction with your voice are keys to making an effective telephony greeting.

[All clients want] "The Professional Sound." It's something I hear all the time: "A smooth delivery, with a bright voice." They generally don't want a radio announcer voice. Female voices are generally chosen ten to one for telephony greetings. The general, chauvinistic opinion is that female voices are more soothing and pleasant. On the other hand, male voices tend to be chosen for technical specification, financial information, or anywhere a serious tone is needed. As a company, we try to break out of the box with our writing and the style of our talent. But clients do not always want that. More than half the time they want the same message cadence and delivery they hear everywhere. Even then, we try to put a spin on it.

We try to avoid the stupid standard script lines like, "Your call is important, please remain on the line," and "Your call will be answered in the order received." All the research we have done indicates that callers are turned off by these overused statements and they offer no purpose today. Time is a valuable commodity. Don't cloud your message with wasteful statements.

As for new talent, we accept demos from anyone interested in doing voice work. We are always looking for voice talent. In almost twenty years of searching for talent, we've found that a majority of people who say they are interested never send a demo. Nine times out of ten, people who actually do send a demo never follow up! Unless their demo was spectacular, we usually don't call them. There's a lesson here: Follow up. It's not always the quality of a demo that keeps us from calling someone; often we just don't have time to call new talent. So be persistent. Make phone calls, send e-mails. It's true what they say about the squeaky wheel.

Once we do accept a talent, we tend to work together for many years. We generally look for actors who can do a fast turnaround and give a good read the first time. They must have an understanding of the script, and the usual voice qualities of good talent—professional sound and a really smooth delivery—are always in demand.

Audiobooks and New Media

5

- Nonfiction audiobooks
- What's new in audiobooks?
- Podcasting
- Media convergence
- Voice for Hire: Patrick Fraley

Audiobooks are a hot commodity these days, and a small group of men and women are working at the highest level of audiobook recording, voicing the big blockbuster novels that often make their way to bestseller lists. Their styles and voices vary, but what they have in common, according to long-time audiobook producer Claudia Howard of Recorded Books in New York City, is a common background in the stage-acting community. "They have been trained and have a lot of experience in words, language, literature, and poetry, and they can handle the huge amount of text that is involved in reading a book out loud," she says. "They know character creation. Many of them are extremely skilled in mimicry and regional and foreign accents, and they know how to use their imagination to create living people with their voices."

NONFICTION AUDIOBOOKS

Randy has recorded several audiobooks. Her first was Dr. Laura Schlessinger's *Ten Stupid Things Women Do to Mess Up Their Lives.* Her second foray into the literary world called upon her to co-narrate the book called *The Most Brilliant Thoughts of All Time (In Two Lines or Less).*

For Dr. Laura's book, Randy worked three days a week for about four weeks, recording in three- and four-hour sessions. (It's worth noting that it generally takes two to three times longer to edit an audiobook reading than it does to record it.) Dr. Laura had already recorded an abridged version of the book, and Randy's recording was geared to fans who wanted to hear more of the book than what Dr. Laura's schedule would allow her to record.

Randy had listened to Dr. Laura long before she met her, so she knew that Dr. Laura's radio talk show style was no-nonsense. Randy was very clear about how she thought the book should sound. She chose to give the callers to Dr. Laura's show who are quoted in the book a sincere yet dispassionate read; she did not want to make them seem like victims, though many were. Randy wanted listeners to come to that conclusion themselves. Depending on the tone of Dr. Laura's response, Randy would deliver her words of advice in a warm, authoritative tone or sometimes in a terse manner.

What's New?

On many fronts, opportunities for artists with good voice-over skills are growing. In audiobooks, according to Claudia Howard of Recorded Books, the latest big trend is downloads. Users are able to log on to websites, purchase an audiobook online, and download it to a computer. From there they are able to load the audiobook onto an MP3 player or burn it onto CDs they can carry with them. "That means we will probably see lots of new audio being produced," says Claudia, "and be it audiobooks or online magazines and newspapers, websites galore will start to offer audio content. We're going to see an increase in opportunity for vocal actors." This is especially welcome news, Claudia says, because "there has been an enormous amount of talent out there, and not necessarily all that many audiobook productions. So, in the past, breaking into the audiobook industry has been as diffi-cult as landing a role on Broadway or getting into another part of the voice-over world."

PODCASTING

The term podcasting derives its name from Apple's iPod, but it refers in general to a type of online media delivery in which digital media files can be distributed over the Internet and played back on portable media players and personal computers.

With podcasting you can create any content of your choosing, so what you create is as varied as the subjects that interest you. Whatever the subject, the most important element you can bring to a podcast is your passion and distinct approach.

Voice actor Erin Lucas studied voice-over with Peter and Randy several years ago in an effort to get closer to her dream of becoming a VJ for MTV. Her desire to be on-camera meant she needed to become a better communicator, so she studied voice-over to be better able to pick up a piece of copy and read it well and on the fly.

> "Websites galore will start to offer audio content. We're going to see an increase in opportunity for vocal actors."
> —Claudia Howard, Recorded Books

Not long after she completed voice-over training, Erin began doing podcast-style reports on the fashion industry in New York City for the site PodcastGO.com. On this website, consumers can download short videos on health, cooking, fashion, money management, and other topics. In her role as fashion reporter Erin researched, interviewed, and narrated her stories during New York's fashion week. Since then, Erin has been an episode participant on *AMC Date Night* and is now the news correspondent for www.jimbreuer.com (her show is "Breuniverse News with Erin Lucas") and has representation on both coasts.

MEDIA CONVERGENCE

Some observers say that media convergence—the ability to inter-change text, audio, and visual communication over the Internet—has been the most significant development in the news industry in the past century. Formerly unseen writers are being thrust into the streets to report their stories. They capture the visuals on tape, write and narrate an accompanying storyline, and upload the file into cyberspace, where the story is immediately accessible across the globe within moments after the event actually happened. In this medium, the writer's voice must tell the story. Who would have thought just a few years ago that news reporters would be broadcasting breaking news stories from their laptops? What this means for you as a voice-over artist is that you have new ways to bring words to life and express yourself.

Voice for Hire: Patrick Fraley

Pat Fraley, a talented and experienced Voice for Hire, has a long list of credits as a narrator and performer in the field of audiobooks. Pat has also supplied voices for more than 4,000 cartoons, placing him among TV animation's top ten performers of all time. He has taught voice for thirty-two years, is a member of Voice and Speech Trainers of America (VASTA), and holds a master of fine arts degree in acting from Cornell University. Pat shares some of his secrets for doing audiobook narration.

I read the book with an eye and ear out for the "author's voice." I'm looking for the author's point of view and how I might realize that with my voice. I adjust my voice in some way. Frank Muller, who Stephen King called "the Valentino of readers," told me once that he never changes his voice unless he has to. I guess I never use my own voice unless I have to. I usually adjust my voice to something that aligns with and realizes the author's main narration "character."

I record in sequence. If I'm bouncing from character to character, with the "he says," and "she saids," sometimes there are pauses and false starts. But hey, that's what editing is for! When I performed the audiobook of *The Adventures of Huckleberry Finn* (there are more than a hundred characters in that evergreen classic!), I had thirteen men on a raft, all interacting. I think you can hear Nixon on that raft.

I'm comfortable with characters who sound like they fell out of a French farce, and I read books that call for full-on pedal-to-the-metal characterization. I've been fortunate to receive good notices and awards for many of the books I've read, but no one is beating down my door to read Proust. I know my limitations (apparently I didn't receive the subtle gene) and flaunt them. I also mine Northwestern and Midwestern authors and literature, as I know the people, the landscape, and the dialects . . . another talent that I ride like an old pony.

When I portray women and girls, I play the character traits and not the female deal—nobody wants to imagine me in seamed stockings! Often, I will actually be lower (in pitch) than the men. Oh, I might add a bit of breath to a female character if it's appropriate, but that's a tiger pit to avoid.

I never read more than three or four hours at a time. I can't. That's why I produce the projects I read. That way I can set the session times and work around other jobs and auditions. I know people who can read forever. As far as the total time I will spend recording the book, it's a simple formula: You read a page of the book, with mistakes, and multiply by the number of pages. Bingo!

Animation

- The growing field
- Building Your Repertoire
- Learning to use your body
- How to know if animation is right for you
- Animation bookings and auditions
- Video games
- Exercises: Make a Sketch and Developing your character repertoire
- Voice for Hire: Mike Pollock

Crazy voices. You do them for friends, relatives, coworkers, and sometimes for yourself. It's a whole lot of fun to clown around. But do you have what it takes to use these voices for profit? Perhaps. It all begins with talent. Voice-over training cannot give you a great ear or the gift of mimicry. What it can do is help you hone and define unique and original character voices that may lead to an exciting extension of your voice-over career.

ANIMATION TODAY

Animation covers a much broader spectrum of voice-over opportunities than it once did. Advancements in computer graphics and computer generated imagery (CGI) have made animation a regular staple of the movies. Consider *Toy Story, Finding Nemo, Shrek,* and *The Incredibles,* to name but a few. While it's true that most of the lead characters of these animated feature films are recognizable celebrity voices, these movies also create opportunities for noncelebrity actors in sequels, spin-offs, pull-string toys, and video games. Saturday morning cartoons continue to feature a wide array of animated characters to entertain America's youth—from superheroes and villains to talking animals and inanimate objects—and a good number of prime-time series geared toward adult audiences (*The Simpsons, Family Guy, King of the Hill*) are animated.

Then, of course, there are the puppets. The *Sesame Street* family of voice artists and puppeteers have been brilliantly educating, entertaining, and enriching the lives of children everywhere for decades. Some of the most endearing characters of our time have been created and performed by pioneer puppeteer and voice artist Jim Henson and the talented puppeteers who worked for him. Can you imagine a world without Kermit the Frog, Cookie Monster, Miss Piggy, or Elmo? Just the mention of Kermit's name conjures up that trademark, quirky, rounded, back-of-the-throat sound that Henson made legendary. Without voices, though, these characters are just vacant inanimate objects: It's the voice artist's responsibility to bring his or her character to life.

IS ANIMATION RIGHT FOR YOU?

Today's animation market requires the voice artist to be a highly versatile performer, with the ability to play it over the top or very real and grounded. Your performance will vary depending upon the writers' intentions, their target audience, and what they're looking for in the character. It behooves you as the aspiring animation actor to hone your repertoire of characters so that each of them is distinctive and three-dimensional.

Keep in mind, though, that animation is not a field that every voice artist needs to try! But animation may be for you

- if you constantly make your friends laugh
- if you've always been drawn to doing impersonations of people, celebrities, or cartoon characters
- if you have the ability to completely change your voice
- if you have a great ear for languages, accents, dialects, and regionalisms.

Just because you enjoy watching cartoons and animated features doesn't mean that you will break into this very competitive niche market. Before you spend time and money producing an animation reel, ask yourself honestly and perhaps those who know you best if this indeed an innate talent of yours. If the answer is yes, then here are some ways to pursue this dream.

BUILDING YOUR REPERTOIRE

Different vocal qualities should capture different characters in a recognizable way. Characters, after all, range in style, sound, age, region, gender, accent, and intelligence, and their vocal qualities can also exhibit range from high to very low, gruff to round, hushed to loud, textured to smooth. For instance, if you're portraying a ditzy starlet from 1940s film noir, her voice is probably going to be high-pitched and even nasal. If you're portraying a mob boss, he might have a New York accent. He also might speak quietly because he's so powerful that he doesn't need to shout to command respect. Animated characters' physical characteristics are typically exaggerated—big noses, droopy ears, big hair, prominent chins, etc.—so your vocal choices should also be somewhat exaggerated.

PHYSICALITY

Your body, from head to toe, is an instrument. In order to play good music, you must first learn how to play the instrument. Never allow the confines of a voice-over booth, no matter how small it may be, to inhibit you. Your arms, shoulders, fingers, knees, and hips can accentuate what you do as an actor, and let's not forget the face: There are more muscles in the human face than in the rest of the entire human body. That should give you some indication of the degree to which you can work your facial muscles to manipulate your voice, which is, after all, also a physical entity. No one cares what you look like in the booth. Frankly, no one is watching, including you.

> "You usually leave a lung and some blood on the window."
> —Michael Bell, animation voice-over artist

ANIMATION AUDITIONS

Most animation auditions are facilitated by casting directors who contact talent agents with specifications (or "specs") for a character in an upcoming movie, a television program, a video game, or other animated work. These specs consist of a verbal description of the character ("Bart Simpson is a mischievous twelve-year-old who constantly plays pranks on his dysfunctional father and younger sister") and sometimes a black-and-white rendering showing age, height, weight, posture, ethnicity, species, texture (feathers, acne, horns, claws, etc.). Visual sketches are extremely helpful for the voice artist as he or she prepares for the audition. Often, they show the character from different angles or experiencing different emotions (sobbing, laughing, etc.), giving the voice artist more insight into the character's demeanor and personality and more clues into what that character's voice should sound like.

The agents then select from their client rosters the animation artists they think are suitable for the roles being cast, fax the specs to the actors they've selected, and schedule audition appointments with the casting directors.

You'll audition for the casting director by reading dialogue with another auditioning actor or just "wild lines" (isolated lines of dialogue taken directly from the script) in the original voice(s) you have created. Casting directors tend to work you for a bit of time in the booth during an animation audition: If you have gotten an audition, you have been highly recommended by your talent agency in what is a small and competitive marketplace. You'll probably be asked to make adjustments (in order to give the producer a variety of different voices to choose from) or even to read for other roles—after all, hiring Hank Azaria to play Apu, Moe, Chief Wiggum, Lou, Carl, and the Comic Book Guy is much more efficient and cost-effective for the producers of *The Simpsons* than having to find, schedule, and pay individual actors to voice each of those characters. Luckily, it also results in more money for the voice artist!

ANIMATION BOOKINGS

In many instances, an animation booking is the best kind of voice-over booking you can attain, since many animated voice-over jobs are long-term gigs.

New technologies are changing the way the animation genre works. In order to cut costs and increase efficiency, many of today's largest animation houses will record their voices in isolation, so you might record your part of a back-and-forth dialogue without the other voice actor being present. In some cases, especially with celebrity talent, the voice actor may not even be in the same city as the director or engineer. For instance, Mike Myers, who voices Shrek, was able to record all his scenes from a home studio, allowing him to continue working on other projects. If you are working alone when recording animation, make sure the director is very clear and concise in his or her acting notes and can verbalize each intricate storyline to help you bring characters to life.

THE VIDEO-GAME MARKET

The video-game market is a billion-dollar industry employing thousands of voice artists. Video games are so complex and require so many voices that one single video game may employ hundreds of voice actors—take a look at the credits of a video game to see just how many voice actors some of these games employ—and if you ever look at the shelves at your local video games store, you can see there is no shortage of games being produced. Indeed, this marketplace is growing as games can be played on a variety of different home systems, personal computers, and portable game consoles.

Video games today are basically interactive movies, with characters who range from the everyday to the absurd. Accents, dialects, and regionalisms all help to paint the world in which the game takes place. The dialogue for many games is recorded prior to the creation of the graphic elements. Therefore, your vocal performance can make a huge impact on the way your character is animated and seen. In addition, it is your job to maintain consistency and specificity in the way your characters speak, feel, and emote. Nothing will upset a voice director more than altering the way your character speaks and acts from one session to another. The integrity of your character must stay true to the writer's intentions, just as in any storyline you would see in a film, television program, or play.

In essence, this line of character work is all about the acting. It is essential that you, the voice actor, provide a wide vocal range and

Exercise
Make a Sketch

You may not be a graphic artist, but simply sketching your character's likeness on a page is a helpful device. Looking at a graphic representation of your character will help you zero in on the correct vocal qualities, pitch, tone, speed, and rhythm for your character. You can take the game further by creating three other voices for the same drawing. This gives you options, and you can decide which voice fits the bill best.

---

limitless imagination, but at the same time, you must also discern how your character reacts to his or her surroundings, predicaments, and interactions with other characters.

All this, of course, can be quite grueling, yet rewarding, for the voice-over artist who enjoys acting. As Michael Bell, animation voice-over artist, explains, "You usually leave a lung and some blood on the window, yet I have been fortunate to play all kinds of characters without sitting in a makeup chair getting lathered, powdered, and teased, then stuck into some itchy costume."

With video games, every possible variation of the story must be recorded and produced, based on the player's progress through the game, because the player dictates the story. In the most complicated games being produced today, such as Rockstar's *Grand Theft Auto* series or Valve's *Half-Life* series, nonplayer characters react dynamically to the player's actions. This includes everything from shrieks of pain, sighs of delight, crying, laughing, and complicated narrative exposition. Sports games like EA Sports's *Madden NFL* series provide numerous voice-over jobs for play-by-play announcers and athletes.

If you read a video-game script, much of it is unintelligible on the page unless you know the context in which each line is spoken. It's the director's job to inform the voice actor about what each line of dialogue is in reaction to. Video games are a challenging medium in which to work, but they may be the most rewarding. Your voice, your character, your dialogue, and your reactions all make a huge contribution to the fully produced and fully interactive experience.

Exercise
Developing Your Character Repertoire

Spend some time by yourself in a room with a recording device. There you can bounce off the walls and play, and no one can judge or critique your experimental creativity. Make a list on paper of all the voices you think your body and voice can muster up. Try to include original characters as well as existing cartoon characters and impersonations.

Say whatever comes to your mind as you envision each character. Write or improvise short scripts or catchphrases. Create dialogue between characters. Try to make yourself laugh. Engage physically, not just vocally. In some cases, men can play women and women can play men. Animation, in fact, is the only genre of voice work that can shatter the gender-specific mold. You always want to create characters that are unique, interesting, and entertaining.

By the end of this exercise, you should have broken a sweat. Bear in mind, you should never attempt to do a character voice that does not feel completely comfortable. If you are straining, feeling pain, or getting hoarse, stop immediately. Make note of which voices feel and sound right to your ear. If they do not feel correct, then you should abandon trying to do them for fear that you may create vocal damage that can cut your voice-over career short.

Original Characters/Types
Men

Alien; baby; billionaire; bully; cowboy; hillbilly; jock; leprechaun; mad scientist; mafioso; nerd; oaf; old man; pirate; precocious kid; spoiled brat; sports announcer; stuffy professor; superhero; surfer dude.

Women

Baby; ditzy starlet; ingenue; mom; nerdy girl; old lady; schoolteacher; space alien; spoiled brat; toddler; Valley girl; vamp; witch.

Existing Characters
Great! Now, let's voice existing cartoon characters.

Men

Barney Rubble; Barney the Dinosaur; Beavis; Bert; Big Bird; Bugs Bunny; Butthead; Charlie the Starkist Tuna; Cookie Monster; Daffy Duck; Donald Duck; Elmer Fudd; Elmo; Ernie; Foghorn Leghorn; Fred Flintstone; the Geico Gecko; Goofy; Grover; Homer Simpson; Kermit the Frog; Lucky Charms Leprechaun; Marvin the Martian; Mickey Mouse; Oscar the Grouch; Peter Griffin (from *Family Guy*); Pluto; Popeye; Porky Pig; Scooby Doo; Stewie Griffin (from *Family Guy*); the Trix Rabbit; Tony the Tiger; Toucan Sam.

Women

Abby Cadabby; Ariel the Little Mermaid; Babs (from *Animaniacs*); Baby Bop; Barbie; Bart Simpson; Betty Boop; Cinderella; Cruella de Vil; Daisy Duck; Dot (from *Animaniacs*); Jessica Rabbit; Lisa Simpson; Lucy Van Pelt; Marge Simpson; Minnie Mouse; Miss Piggy; Mulan; Olive Oyl; Peggy Hill; Peppermint Patty; Pocahontas; Prairie Dawn; Sally Brown; Snow White; Snuggles Bear; Ursula the Sea Witch.

Impressions

Now try imitating real people. People you grew up with. Family members. Neighbors. Colleagues and friends. Many of your most original characters will come directly from your personal experiences with these folks. Also, try to imitate some celebrities. A good impersonation can land you work in both commercial voice-over and animation voice-over. In some cases, however, an impersonation or imitation that falls short and sounds nothing like its intended subject can often be the birth of an entirely new character that belongs to you and only you.

Men

Andy Rooney; Bela Lugosi; Bill Clinton; Cary Grant; Charles Bronson; Christopher Walken; Dan Rather; Dr. Phil; Elvis Presley; George Foreman; Gerald Ford; Jack Nicholson; James Cagney; Jerry Lewis; Jimmy Carter; Jimmy Stewart; Joe Pesci; John F. Kennedy; Keanu Reeves; Marlon Brando; Marv Albert; Mike Tyson; Muhammad Ali; Peter Lorre; Presidents Bush 41 and 43; Richard Nixon; Ronald Reagan; Sammy Davis Jr.; Sylvester Stallone; Vin Scully; Woody Allen.

Women

Barbara Walters; Barbra Streisand; Bette Davis; Bette Midler; Celine Dion; Cher; Connie Chung; Dame Judi Dench; Eleanor Roosevelt; Ellen DeGeneris; Ethel Merman; Hillary Clinton; Jennifer Lopez; Joan Crawford; Joan Rivers; Judy Garland; Julia Child; Julie Andrews; Katharine Hepburn; Kathleen Turner; Lily Tomlin; Liza Minnelli; Madonna; Mae West; Margaret Thatcher; Martha Stewart; Nancy Grace; Queen Elizabeth; Rosie Perez; Wanda Sykes; Whoopi Goldberg; Zsa Zsa Gabor.

Voice for Hire: Mike Pollock

For years, voice actor Mike Pollock has been working with 4Kids Entertainment, the company that has produced popular animated cartoons for Fox Television's 4Kids TV programming (formerly the FoxBox). Mike can currently be heard as the narrator of Pokemon *as well as a host of animated characters for* Ultimate Muscle, Sonic X, Kirby: Right Back At Ya!, Teenage Mutant Ninja Turtles, Yu-Gi-Oh!, *and* Yu-Gi-Oh! The Movie. *Mike also voices the promos for all of these shows and more. Here's a glimpse into a day in the life of a working animation voice actor.*

At 4Kids, once you get past the audition process and are fortunate enough to get cast, your life is ruled by the fine folks at Talent Central. They're responsible for booking all the talent and acting as a liaison between producers and talent. They usually book a week at a time, so by Thursday or Friday, you'll hear from them with their plans for you for the following week. After a little give-and-take, you work out a schedule that works for everyone involved.

4Kids usually dubs cartoons it has acquired from another country into English in a process called automated dialogue replacement (ADR), in which each line is replaced one at a time. Typically, you show up at the studio and are handed a script. There's rarely an opportunity to pre-read or otherwise prepare, so being able to cold-read confidently is always a plus. You head into the booth, slap on a pair of headphones, and spend the next hour or two trying to stare simultaneously at a screen and a script, while performing and taking direction from a director and an engineer behind the glass.

In a nutshell, the goal of ADR is to be able to read the line to match the on-screen character's lip-flap timing while still sounding convincing. Perhaps the oddest thing you have to get used to with ADR is the beeping. Before you record each line, you hear a series of three beeps in your headphones. They let you know when to speak. When the beeps stop beeping, you start speaking. You watch the screen and the script, trying to match flap, sometimes hearing the other actors, if they've already recorded, or reacting to nothing. After each take, the director will either say, "That's great!" or give some kind of direction to adjust the performance or some technical note, like, "We had a little noise in there," or "You banged the copy stand. Do it again!"

When you're done, the real magic happens. The engineer will massage your last take in ProTools, squeezing, stretching, editing, tweaking until it fits just right. In most cases, the director is extremely helpful, especially since he or she is much more familiar with the material than you are and knows what the producer wants. After you're done with your initial session, you may be called back in to do fixes if a producer heard something odd or rewrote a line and stuff has to be re-recorded. Between three and six months later, you'll see what you did on TV.

There is one exception in the 4Kids lineup: *Teenage Mutant Ninja Turtles* is done as a pre-lay (voices recorded before the animation is created). In other words, all—or at least most—of the actors record as an ensemble. You also get the advantage of seeing the script a few days in advance. When you arrive in the morning, the cast will do a table read. As the name suggests, you sit around a table and read! It gives you a chance to familiarize yourself with the material and work out any kinks. After a quick break, it's into the studio. Usually, four or five actors record together, with other cast members wandering in and out as the session goes on. In the case of *TMNT,* the director is off-site. You only hear her over headphones, while producers and the engineer maintain a local presence on the other side of the glass from you. While recording separately in ADR has its advantages—like privacy and fewer people getting pissed when you screw up—ensemble recording has its advantages, too. You really feel like you're part of a big production, and you can play off other actors, for more authentic reactions. There's one other real big advantage. Although it takes up to nine months to see the finished product, it's cool to know that the animation was actually based on your performance. Once the episode is animated, you might be called back in for fixes, if necessary.

Live Announcing

- Announcing awards shows
- Randy's first-hand account of announcing the Academy Awards
- Announcing game shows
- Voice for Hire: Randy West
- Voice for Hire: Ken Levine

The live announcer is the voice you hear during a live broadcast, such as awards shows (the Oscars, the Emmys, the Tonys, the Grammys) or game shows (*The Price Is Right*). What makes announcing markedly different from studio work is the fact that you have only one chance to get it right. That is why very few successful voice-over artists want to do live announcing. Most of them say, "Who needs it?" The ability to deliver a flawless performance under extreme circumstances is a highly specialized talent.

In 1993, Randy became the first woman chosen to announce the Academy Awards. She has also been the announcer for the Tony Awards and many other live awards shows. The following includes her accounts of working these live shows.

A LITTLE HISTORY

The producers of major, nationally televised awards shows are known to play it safe when it comes to the role of the announcer. They tend to go with the known quantity, the proven formula of an offstage announcer who has done it before and can deliver a near-flawless performance under incredible pressure.

Most television producers choose an experienced professional announcer because a big part of the job is to move the show along in a smooth and timely fashion. We asked Gil Cates, a producer of the Academy Awards, how he chooses an announcer:

> Personally, I prefer a female voice. I find it nurturing and pleasant. I was concerned about how advertisers and the network would react when we had our first female voice on the Oscars. Randy did a terrific job, and we had no negative comments. Not one. Quite unusual, I thought.
>
> Randy's professionalism and intelligence are the unique qualities that have brought her back to the Oscars numerous times. She has learned to think of her job and her job only . . . a terrific quality, and one that I admire, especially in an Academy Awards announcer, who must be smart and a team player. He or she must be willing to work hard and prepare. Preparation is the key to success in anything, and announcing a TV broadcast requires intense preparation and concentration.

Live announcing is like a reenactment of Daniel in the lion's den. Will your faith in your ability enable you to get it right from the page to the live audience? Or will you falter and be devoured by the lions? The lions in this scenario are the director, producers, critics, and your peers. Should you ever be lucky enough to be chosen to announce this type of broadcast event, put your own stamp on this special opportunity.

RANDY AT THE AWARD SHOWS

It happened that 1993 was the Year of the Woman. Needless to say, I was thrilled beyond belief to be sitting in my booth at the Academy Awards perched on the edge of my seat for what would be the most thrilling three hours of my life. As a first-timer and as the first woman to ever announce this type of program, I was over the moon! Since that evening, female announcers have gained some ground in popularity and have become a regular part of broadcast event programming.

My career in awards shows began when Danette Arden, executive in charge of talent for the Oscars, heard my voice on the radio. Danette had her producer, Gil Gates, listen to my tape, and he passed it on to

Some Excerpts from Randy's Oscar Blog

As one of the announcers of the 80th Annual Academy Awards show, I had a nine-day whirlwind experience in February 2008. Here are some excerpts from the blog that appeared on my website, www.randythomasvo.com.

In January, I got the call from director Louis J. Horvitz inviting me back to the Academy Awards. He told me that I would be co-announcing with Tom Kane, a veteran voice-over artist. This was Tom's second time behind the microphone at the Oscars.

Thankfully, ten days before the broadcast, the Writers Guild of America settled their strike and the writers went back to work. It was announced that Jon Stewart was going to host and the big show would go on as hoped.

Tom and I shared an area about the size of a large closet. It was perhaps six by six feet. And it was located in the back of the orchestra mixing trailer. Tom and I were not alone, thankfully. We had Tina Cannizzaro DeBone with us. Tina is a pro, and her job as script coordinator is to write the winner walk-up copy and check all the facts of each winner for accuracy and also timing. If the nominees are sitting in the first few rows of the Kodak Theater during the show, they will make it to the stage too quickly for anything elaborate or drawn out to be read. Tina always writes her copy in a way

another producer, Jeff Margolis. Before long, they informed me I was the choice. This breakthrough, as you might imagine, was memorable for me and something new for TV audiences.

Awards Shows

A show like the Academy Awards or the Emmys consists of more than twenty-five awards, plus commercials and entertainment, delivered in three hours (and hopefully less). On most awards shows, the announcer is usually the first voice the viewing audience hears. The announcer introduces the host or hostess, as well as the presenters, and voices the sponsorship "billboard copy" in a style that promotes the advertising sponsors, who pay vast sums of money to air thirty-second commercials during an awards broadcast. Announcers also read the copy (script)

that when we are reading it, we can stop halfway through and the facts will still make sense. Tina gives us hand signals to speed up or slow down as we speak. In between acts during the commercial breaks, she also gave Tom and me a quick rundown of the next act so we would feel even more prepared as we came out of the commercial break.

All was going well for me until we got to the award for best animated short film. I rehearsed the possible winners in a low voice, carefully enunciating Maciek Szerbowski (mah-sheck) (tcher-BOW-ski), Samuel Touneux (tour-neuh), Simone Vanesse (si-mon) (van-ness), Alexander Petrof (pe-TROF). Sure enough, the last nominees won and for the *first time* I said the names, reading ahead as I spoke. They were Suzy Templeton and Hugh Welchman. I saw the word "man" in Welchman and I accidentally said Suzy TempleMAN. I instantly knew I said it wrong and knew that if I said nothing the world would not know I had made a mistake. But, I knew that she would! This woman had just won an Academy Award and I wanted to make this moment perfect for her, so I backtracked and quickly said Temple-TON and Hugh Welch-Man. It seems everyone I know heard my little flub. Oh well! As my daughter says, "That's live television!" It was my only flub of the night, and I had a lot of foreign names to pronounce!

highlighting the nominees ("Hilary Swank, *Million Dollar Baby*") and, when the winner is announced, voice his or her walk to the stage with interesting personal and professional tidbits, known as "winner walk-up copy" ("This is Hilary Swank's second Academy Award. She won her first Academy Award at the tender young age of twenty-four in 1999 for *Boys Don't Cry*").

Preproduction can take days or even weeks to complete, even for the "live" announcer. There are three phases from beginning to end: the prerecord session(s), the rehearsal process, and the live show.

The Prerecord Session
Anything that will ultimately be married to a graphic on screen—such as the opening segment, in which we see the names of stars and presenters

along with the show's logo—is prerecorded. The commercial sponsor billboards (where the announcer says "blah, blah, blah is brought to you by Ford or Revlon or American Express") are customarily prerecorded as well. Sometimes the announcer also records the audio for the nomination packages. These are the segments in which the presenters on stage say, "The nominees are . . ." and the audience sees a clip of the star or film or hears a snippet of music, depending on the type of show. The director and crew can use the prerecording of the nominee package during the rehearsal process to determine the timing of that segment.

The prerecord session is your best shot at setting the style and tempo for the show. You can set a style that you will match when you do your live announcing. If you don't match the prerecorded segments with the live announcing, the prerecorded material will sound canned and it will seem like you are using two different voices. To match your voice, though, during the prerecord sessions you must take into consideration what happens to you emotionally and vocally when you go live. Your voice tends to move upward in pitch when you get nervous or excited.

> "People are sometimes surprised at how much I look like I am dancing when I am recording for a show."
> —Randy Thomas, first woman to announce the Academy Awards

People are sometimes surprised at how much I look like I am dancing when I am recording for a show. My hands are moving all the time, as though I were leading an orchestra. I get my energy from this movement, though I am careful not to move my body or feet so I remain in perfect position relative to the microphone.

The Rehearsal

The quality and number of rehearsal days are directly proportionate to the budget for the show, as well as the time limitations of the presenters. For the Oscars, rehearsals last four to five days (not including prerecord dates). The Emmy Awards show rehearses for three or four days, and Broadway's Tony Awards rehearse only on the day of the live broadcast, because the actors appearing in the show are working six days a week.

When you arrive at the venue, the first thing you must do is get your credentials. Your backstage pass is your most valuable possession. This has always been standard operating procedure, even more so after September 11, when every major award show where celebrities are in attendance has security precautions similar to those at the White House. You cannot go five feet without the proper credentials hanging around your neck. Once you have your ID, you head to the stage area and check in with the stage manager. He or she will then turn you over to someone from the sound department, who escorts you to your booth.

The announce booth is usually sequestered away from the hustle and bustle of the stage in a fairly quiet area; it's often a trailer or dressing room that has been converted into an audio booth. Live announce is undeniably prestigious, but the actual job is far from glamorous. You sit in a trailer, usually alone, with a television monitor, microphone, a set of headphones, and a control box with two buttons to press. One button connects you to the show's director. The other connects you to "the world." You need to master the few buttons that enable you to turn your microphone on and off and to go back and forth effortlessly between speaking to the director and to the audience. It is an extremely good idea never to forget which button is which! Your headset is split into left and right channels, so you hear the show live in one ear and the director and assistant director calling your cues live in the other ear. Separate volume knobs allow you to control the volume input for each ear, and finding the perfect audio balance for these two elements takes time and practice.

Upon arrival, you're handed a copy of the script to mark up during rehearsal(s). You'll use it to follow along page by page, word by word, as the show progresses. The show is often rehearsed out of sequence. It progresses act by act but not necessarily in order for various reasons.

It would be preferable to do the show in order, obviously, but talent isn't always available at the time their act is being done. Also, if there's a live orchestra, all their material is done together, to accommodate their breaks and meals. During rehearsal, it can be tedious and taxing to remain on page, but you must remain calm and patient. It is impera- tive that the director, camera, effects, tape people, and stagehands as well as the host and presenters go through the show step by step and moment by moment in rehearsal. When live show time finally rolls around, you will be extremely grateful to have had the opportunity to run your lines in rehearsal, just to have had the practice of vocalizing your part numerous times as the various elements of the show come together in a painstaking, sometimes disorganized and frenetic manner, with a lot of yelling and screaming in your headset (not at you, of course!).

During rehearsals, a team of extras plays the different celebrities and nominees who will be present during the actual show. They are so in character that when their respective names are announced, as in, "and the winner is, for this rehearsal only . . . Julianne Moore!" the woman playing Julianne jumps out of her seat and hugs the person next to her and maybe gets a hug or two from her costars, director, producer, screenwriter, costume designer, or composer seated nearby as she makes her way to the stage. The announcer practices reading the winner walk-up copy. All the while the director is calling camera cues to find anyone in the audience who would have a relationship to the actor or the film/show/CD, etc., for which the actor has just won the award. The director is calling the cues to switch at any moment, depending on whom the actor mentions during his or her acceptance speech. The stand-in actors who are hired to do this work are all very talented and know their jobs so well you can feel the emotion from them as they accept the award as that actor.

> "I feel that I truly get the most out of performance by looking and feeling like I am at the party with everyone else."
> —Randy Thomas

By show time, you have seen and rehearsed a scenario for almost every conceivable winner in all categories. On the day of show, after the final run-through, the stand-in actors are dismissed. The days and hours of rehearsal can seem tedious and sometimes excruciatingly slow. However, when it is time to go live and your voice is heard by millions of people (in the case of the Academy Awards), you are grateful for every moment you have had to practice the words you must read. In fact, you may wish there was even more time to get it perfect.

The Live Show

On the day of the big show you wake up (that is, if you actually slept the night before) feeling nervous and excited. There is a full dress rehearsal on this day, so you have one last chance to go through the entire show. This run-through happens in show order (perhaps for the first time). After the final run-though on the day of the show, the director calls a lunch break, and it is during this time that everyone must do whatever it is they need to do to prepare for going live to the world.

One question I am often asked is how I am dressed during the show. It is assumed that since I am heard and not seen that I am dressed in casual clothing. As if! Actually, one of the best things about announcing the Academy Awards, Emmy Awards, and Tony Awards is that I can dress in my finest clothes. I feel that I truly get the most out of my performance by looking and feeling like I am at the party with everyone else who is there. I choose my outfits very carefully, knowing that I will be out on the red carpet and also going to a ball and parties after the show. Standing next to Gwyneth Paltrow or Oprah Winfrey at the Governor's Ball can inspire you to take great care and deliberation in choosing your outfit! I keep in mind how comfortable I will be sitting in this outfit for the entire show and going to the parties afterward and, most important, whether any movement of my arms or body will cause the material of the dress to make a sound. That would be bad news and very unprofessional for someone whose job is all about sound. (As you can imagine, I own a lot of black dresses and pantsuits. Until they invent something darker, I'm sticking with black!)

I like to create a warm and comfortable environment in my booth. It makes me feel good and more relaxed to have certain things around me when I work. Candles, aromatherapy, tea (my tea of choice is called Throat Coat, and it is available at most health food stores). I also like to have a nice teacup. I generally do not eat much during the afternoon of the show, limiting myself to fruit and vegetables, and I make sure in the days before the show to avoid anything that will lower my immune system or interfere with my performance by coating my throat with phlegm—that means no sugar, orange juice, or cheese.

I request dozens of bottles of water, which means I must also be located very close to a bathroom. During the course of the show the announcer speaks every minute or two. Trust me, you do not want to be thinking about the fact that you need to "go" or have to make a long dash to the nearest restroom and make it back to your booth by running a hundred-yard dash and sounding totally winded on the air. So I offer you this tip from experience: If there is only one request you make as the announcer, it is to be located very close to a restroom facility, so you can dash in quickly during a break.

The Red Carpet

In the 1990s, it was the announcer's job to provide the audio coverage of the red carpet arrivals. Today, the networks do their own red carpet pre-shows, spending thirty minutes to an hour showing the world everyone who arrives and what they're wearing. So, the announcer only announces the awards show itself. The announcer's work is thoroughly rehearsed by show time, with one huge exception: At times I have done a red carpet arrival sequence aired during the opening of the show. In these cases, I am given 3 × 5-inch index cards that contain brief copy and are numbered in the order in which we will see quick shots of the stars on the red carpet.

I read through these cards to make sure the copy is fluid and there are no difficult names to pronounce. The copy is written to be short enough to accommodate the three- to five-second shot of each star. You don't want to get caught up reading a long blurb about one star when the video is showing someone else. Playing catch-up by suddenly reading really quickly live on the air makes the announcer sound unprepared. I sometimes mark the cards to show where I will edit the copy myself if I find I am falling behind in the sequence.

I cannot easily look at the screen and read the names of the stars at the same time. So, I sit poised and ready with my index cards in the proper order in my hands, waiting for the director to cue me by tapping me on the shoulder. I then read the first card, toss it, and wait to be tapped on my shoulder again, then immediately read the next card. I hold my position until I feel the next tap, and so on. This is the most unnerving part of the show, and in the vernacular it's "poop-in-your-pants time."

For the 67th Academy Awards, in 1995, I had a production assistant designated as my "tapper." This person was doing this very stressful job for the first time. He was more nervous than I was. Just moments before the show began and I was about to go live for the opening sequence, the director's voice popped on in my headset and told me the cards I was about to read from were not correct. I had one additional person to announce—I was to insert Sharon Stone in front of Jason Alexander. My assistant grabbed the cards to insert the name and accidentally knocked over my water bottle, spilling the contents onto the index cards, the script, and me. I did not even have time at that point to write in Sharon Stone's name in front of Jason Alexander's.

As they counted me in to go live in five, four, three, two, one, I said to my helper, "Never mind, just point to the screen and I'll do it on the fly." I began reading the cards in perfect time to the video of stars parading down the red carpet and had almost forgotten that there was this last-minute change until I read the name Jason Alexander. At that moment my assistant put his hands in front of my eyes and pointed to the screen. I saw that it was indeed Sharon Stone and not Jason Alexander, so I said in a very matter of fact voice, "Of course, that's Sharon Stone . . . and now there's Jason Alexander." I was shaking when I finished reading. The director instantly appeared in my headset to compliment me for being so heads-up and apologized for the last-minute change, promising to never let that happen again.

"And the Winner Is . . . "

Even with seven Academy Awards shows and more than twenty-five other major live broadcasts under my belt, I am still a bundle of nerves until I get through the opening sequence. Then, I am finally able to relax a bit, knowing that I have rehearsed everything else. The fact that these are live shows means that even though you have rehearsed many times, anything, and I mean anything, can happen. The director can call many audibles, and you must be ready for any challenge that may come your way.

The Tony Awards

The Tonys are among the many shows for which I am brought in to rehearse during the day for the live show that very night. Because the actors are live on stage six nights a week, they have no time to come in and rehearse before then. On the day of the 54th Tony Awards at Rockefeller Center in New York City in 2000, the director, producer, and sound man faced so many challenges fine-tuning the performances that they did not notice until we were on the air live that the sound from my booth was hollow and reflective, sort of vaguely echoey and strange-sounding. The problem turned out to be that the dressing room where I was stationed had mirrors on all four walls. During rehearsal I thought to myself that this was not a warm acoustic environment for recording, but no one had said a word to me, so I didn't worry about it.

Near the end of the first hour I saw my cell phone was ringing and realized it was my mother, who lives in Florida (and is glued to her TV for any show I am doing). So I picked up the phone (since I had a five-minute break) and I asked my mother what she thought of the show so far. The tone of her voice was incredulous. She said, "You sound awful!" She continued by saying that I sounded like I was in a tunnel and that every time they brought up the applause it totally drowned me out.

I instantly sprang into action. The control room was in a state of controlled chaos, with lots of set and stage cues and various preparations in motion, so I decided to ask my production assistant to run and grab a stagehand and return with blankets and duct tape to hang over the mirrors to create some sound insulation. She returned two minutes later with blankets and tape but no stagehand. We quickly hung all the blankets and, to add a bit more warmth to my voice, I held my jacket over my head, draping it down around me to catch and stop any reflection of my voice. Sometime during the next part of the show I called my mom once again and she quickly remarked what an amazing difference there was in the sound quality.

After the broadcast I went down to the control truck to congratu-late the director and producer on a great show, and found my sound engineer. I briefly shared the story of what had happened, and he told me they had been aware of the problem and had worked busily during the second hour of the show to remedy the situation. So apparently it was the combination of our efforts that worked like a charm.

The lesson of this story for me is to pay attention to my instincts and question my audio environment while something might still be done about it. Only during the rehearsal process can you get all the bugs out before they haunt you in front of millions of people. That, of course, is the reason for all the run-throughs that take place before a show goes live. My little announcer world is only one small cog in the giant wheel that must be perfect in every way for a live show to be successful.

GAME SHOWS

Why do we love game shows? Because they are both games and shows, two things most people enjoy! The opportunity to quiz, test, challenge, and compete for money brings out the best and the worst in us. Game shows are a test of knowledge and skill, and the contestants' desire to win make them quite exciting and fun for the viewer. Some early game shows, such as *The $64,000 Question,* crashed and burned because of greed and dishonesty within the networks. Thankfully, since then standards and practices have been applied to maintain integrity and keep the playing field and the games honest and fair.

Great game shows have great hosts. Bob Barker, the long-time host of *The Price Is Right,* had audience-participation skills that were unparalleled. Drew Carey, the lucky host chosen to continue to carry *The Price Is Right* torch, will no doubt create his own indelible mark on the show. Even the long-popular show *Wheel of Fortune* floun-dered when Rolf Benirschke took over as host of the daytime version in 1989 when Pat Sajak briefly left, though Sajak's return has ensured the prime-time version is a long-running success.

Along with a great host, a great announcer is also a must. Johnny Olson's "Come on down!!!!" is the signature line that stands out—everyone knows what show that line is from, right? Olson began his game-show announcing career in the late 1940s on the radio. His first TV announcing job was in 1958, on *Name That Tune.* Throughout his career until his death in 1985, Olson announced thirty-two game shows for Mark Goodson–Bill Todman Productions.

Rod Roddy, also a beloved member of the game-show announcer world, succeeded Johnny on *The Price Is Right.* Roddy began announcing game shows in 1979 and was the announcer for shows such as *Whew!, Battlestars, Love Connection, Hit Man,* and *Press Your Luck.* Roddy passed away in 2003, and Rich Fields continues in his footsteps on *The Price Is Right.* The skill and delight of performing for a live studio game-show audience is at the top of the list for today's game-show announcers.

Voice for Hire: Randy West

Randy West is one of the best in the business. If you have ever seen Supermarket Sweep, *you will know Randy as the voice who takes you on a spin around the grocery store with his "and now here she comes, down the frozen food aisle . . . YES! . . ."*

Similar to working on live award shows, the game-show announcer has to be able to concentrate on several things at once, such as listening for the "announce" cue deep in the cacophony of chatter on the headset. The director is in my left ear with his "Standby music, standby lighting, ready camera 1, take camera 1, cue lighting, cue music, tighten 1, standby VT1, standby announce, open the door, ANNOUNCE! ready camera 2, take 2, roll VT1, ready camera 3, cue applause, take 3, FASTER RANDY!, take VT1. . . ."

Meanwhile, in my right ear is the program's audio, so I can hear the host and the music that's accompanying my read. My left arm is flailing wildly over my head as I encourage the audience's applause. One eye is on the copy, and the other is on a monitor. I'm watching to be sure I don't "tip" the prize with an enthusiastic "A new car!" before the camera has the shot and the doors are starting to open for the reveal. Oh, and don't turn to the next page yet, because it'll be my job to extract the make and model of the vehicle from the flowing prose that describes the thrill of the wind in your hair and lists the optional equipment.

Crazy? Sure, but I'm never more alive than when I am in that action. And it's a special adrenaline rush when I glance up to see Bob Barker or Wink Martindale looking at me and ready for a quick verbal volley. You've heard it, "Do you have another contestant for us, Randy," or "Randy, tell us about today's bonus prize." Ad-libbing a quick response to the host such as, "I'm ready with the good news now, Bob," before diving into the scripted copy adds so much to the show's flow, fun, and friendly feeling.

Part of the appeal of game shows for networks, syndicators, and cable nets is that they are among the least expensive shows to produce. Of the major genres of TV program, only talk shows are sometimes less expensive. But game shows are often more attractive because we regularly tape as many as seven episodes in an eight-hour workday. In an era when a single episode of scripted dramatic television regularly costs more than 2 million dollars, an hour of Regis [Philbin] officiating over *Who Wants to Be a Millionaire* has generated champagne ratings on a beer budget. There's nothing sweeter in the eyes of the network "suits."

The presence of an audience contributes to the energy on set and helps the host with pacing. And a live audience requires a warm-up performer to get and keep the crowd responsive. Every game show you ever watched as a child had the program's announcer doubling as the warm-up, and it's a tradition that continues today less for sentimental reasons than as a matter of economics. Where a warm-up performer able to work on a union set might command a $1,000 salary for the day, the antiquated AFTRA code that covers this tiny niche of show business stipulates that if a "cast member" also performs the warm-up responsibility, that performer's added effort can be compensated with an additional minimum scale payment of $50 per episode. Yes, you read that correctly, $50. And other than the host, the announcer is the only other "cast member" on the set.

While it's been years since I was offered a bump of $50 per episode as compensation for the added responsibility, the AFTRA contract has created a long-standing precedent and an expectation that does limit the bargaining position of my brothers and sisters who are proficient at both jobs. Under this pay structure it's always an advantage for a producer to have the announcer/warm-up on set when taping with a live audience rather than hiring a separate warm-up performer. Such is the case with *The Price Is Right, Wheel of Fortune, Jeopardy!,* and the vast majority of game shows.

The game shows I've worked on or am familiar with that have an announcer at all have an announcer who reads live. An exception is one of my favorites among the shows I've enjoyed working on, *Supermarket Sweep.* While it's not common knowledge, the frenetic "play-by-play" of the sweep bonus round where "Betty bounces a bevy of big Butterball birds into her basket" cannot be performed until the video of the sweep is first assembled and edited from the footage recorded by numerous cameras. There's no other effective way to follow the unpredictable action of three teams of manic shoppers simultaneously ravaging a supermarket.

I give each show that I announce a style appropriate to the energy level of the program as I hear it determined by the host, the contestants, the audience, the music, and the audio mix of those elements. Drawing attention to myself at the expense of the content of the show is akin to showing up at a black-tie event wearing a brown leisure suit. My goal is to support and add to the style, pace, and intensity of the program as well as the mood of the moment, be it dramatic expectation or unbridled excitement.

The Price Is Right had an unprecedented thirty-three-year run with only three voices. I saw my job there as presenting a style compatible with and familiar to what the loyal viewers had come to expect. Having been taught the business by that show's original announcer, Johnny Olson, this was an easy task. In fact, Johnny mentored me in the 1970s using his scripts from *The Price Is Right,* complete with his markings for emphasis, phrasing, pace, and flow. I still treasure those scripts from thirty years ago, as well as the encyclopedic knowledge of announcing and warm-up that Johnny generously shared with me. He put a great deal of thought into his seemingly informal and off-the-cuff presentation. Establishing a precedent for how the title and the often-repeated phrases on a new show are delivered and then using those audio signatures consistently are important factors in "branding" the show.

> "Drawing attention to myself at the expense of the content of the show is akin to showing up at a black-tie event wearing a brown leisure suit."
>
> —Randy West, game-show announcer

When the avalanche of "reality" shows started to occupy network time periods and then expand even deeper across the cable landscape, it was looking bleak for the future of game shows. Could a programming genre as old as broadcasting itself actually disappear? Were *Price, Jeopardy!,* and *Wheel* the last of the dinosaurs, with the life form doomed to extinction? I was among the many who were worried.

While the execution and stakes of the games have changed, the basic appeal of game shows hasn't changed, and I doubt it ever will. People are intrigued by watching other regular folks like themselves being challenged, comparing their own instincts with those of the participants, and living vicariously through the successes and failures of others.

Screaming the answer to a *Wheel of Fortune* puzzle in your living room before the contestant has solved it, and feeling the drama as a contestant struggles to answer the final big question on *Who Wants to Be a Millionaire* has the same basic appeal as imagining yourself in the throws of a *Survivor* challenge.

Instead of neon lights providing the "eye candy," the next generation of game shows has something as vast as a tropical island for a backdrop. While the art of producing this next generation of games is vastly different from producing the traditional game show, I think the appeal and the basic plots remain unchanged. While I'll always be nostalgic for the flashing lights, bells, and buzzers, nothing is as constant as change.

Voice for Hire: Ken Levine

Ken Levine is an Emmy-winning writer/director/producer/Major League Baseball announcer. He has been the head writer of *M*A*S*H*, producer of *Cheers,* creative consultant of *Frasier* and *Wings,* voice of the Baltimore Orioles, Seattle Mariners, and San Diego Padres, and currently has a daily blog, www.byKenLevine.com. He is the host of the post-game Dodger Talk on KABC radio.

Every boy has dreams of becoming a big-league ballplayer. Eventually he realizes that the dream will never be. For me that realization came when I was seven. Along with that, I'd always been a radio geek. The idea of a guy talking into an inverted tomato soup can and being heard thousands of miles away (okay, hundreds) intrigued me no end. So it was perfect that the Dodgers moved from Brooklyn to my hometown of Los Angeles when I was eight. I was introduced to their Hall of Fame announcer Vin Scully and it was love at first hear.

"Wow," I thought. "That's the perfect job. You can be on the radio and at a ballgame at the same time! And if you're with a team you also get to travel to exotic locales like Philadelphia in April and St. Louis in August."

I consider myself to be incredibly blessed. My dream came true, but it took time and a very circuitous route. After graduating from UCLA I became a Top 40 disc jockey. For several years I bounced around the country playing "The Night Chicago Died."

Although I still longed to be a baseball announcer, the lure of staying in one city and making good money was too great a pull. I became a TV comedy writer. And even though I was lucky enough to work on some great shows such as *M*A*S*H* and *Cheers,* there was still that nagging desire to really follow my bliss. When I reached my mid thirties I figured it was now or never.

There are no courses in "how to be a baseball announcer" (not even in the DeVry Institute) so I figured the only way to learn was to just do it. For two years I climbed to the upper deck of Dodger Stadium above the timber line and broadcast games into my portable tape recorder. I would then critique my tapes, compare them to actual broadcasts, and I slowly improved to where I wasn't embarrassing myself in front of the drunks and maniacs who populated that section.

A note here about my voice. I hate it. I always wish it were deeper. And yet, my radio career has been more successful than that of hundreds of announcers with deep, rich baritones. How? I figured out the secret. It's simple and irrefutable and crosses all genres.

"Connect with people," is my biggest piece of advice. Really communicate one-to-one with your listener. People don't relate to "broadcasters." They relate to people. Present yourself as real, as someone who has emotions and desires just like they do. That's always been my key. I use humor on the radio. I use humor off the radio. If something strikes me funny on the air I laugh. I react to exciting plays or frustrating plays just the way you would.

That said, there are ways to get the most out of your voice. Along with doing practice games I began seeing a vocal coach. I learned how to really use my voice—how to speak from my diaphragm, how to breathe correctly, how to add variety, shadings, and richness to my instrument (and your voice is an instrument, a finely tuned one). Later I took singing lessons to further my vocal growth. If they ever have *American AARP Idol,* I'll be there belting the crap out of "The Ballad of the Green Berets."

> "There are no courses in 'how to be a baseball announcer' (not even in the DeVry Institute) so I figured the only way to learn was to just do it.
>
> —Ken Levine, writer/producer/director turned
>
> sports announcer

Eventually I sent my play-by-play tape to minor league teams and much to my delight and terror (but mostly delight) I got a call from Syracuse (AAA affiliate of the Toronto Blue Jays). I stayed with them for a year and moved over to Tidewater (the Mets' AAA affiliate) for the next two seasons.

In 1991, I applied for an opening with the Baltimore Orioles and to my astonishment got the job. I had sent them a tape of exciting highlights—home runs, defensive gems, a brushfire set by our fireworks night, etc. They called and asked for additional material. They wanted to hear three uninterrupted innings where nothing happens. Ground outs, walks, pick-off throws to first. They wanted to see how I handled the routine stuff. A number of former players also applied for this job and certainly had more expertise than me, but I was easier and greater fun to listen to. Again, that's the secret.

Thus began a big league career that took me from Baltimore to Seattle to San Diego. It became increasingly difficult to maintain my TV writing career and still be traipsing around the country calling baseball. So ultimately I traded play-by-play in for pre- and post-game shows for the Los Angeles Dodgers. I'm now actually working with Vin Scully.

The job requires preparation, passion, and a seven-month commitment. I have to be at every Dodger game even if they're playing the Pirates. But every time I crack that mic it's thrilling. That rush I got when I first went on the air in Bakersfield, California, in 1971, and had to play Jethro Tull stiffs for burned-out stoners in trailer parks has never left me, never even diminished. There is a special magic to radio that time, technology, or even Clear Channel can't take away. It's still just some schmoe talking into an inverted tomato soup can touching people's lives. But now that schmoe is me.

Trailers

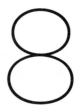

- The big business of trailers
- Landing one of the toughest gigs of all
- Advice from a master coach

You see and hear them in the dark, cool comfort of your local movie theater, while munching on hot, buttered popcorn and Raisinets and sipping a soda: the trailers for the big blockbuster movies, masterful, brilliantly executed campaigns that vie for our future movie dollars.

THE BIG BUSINESS OF TRAILERS

You may have noticed that the few dozen voices you hear doing trailers are male. Why? Primarily because this is the way it's always been done. On average, movies cost $100 million to make, with stars getting $20 million per flick and the publicity folks another $50 million. With money like that at stake, very few studio heads will take a chance on doing something different. The male-voice formula works. However, if a woman should actually break through and voice a successful movie trailer, other studios would most likely follow suit and begin using women as well. Remember, too, that it's tough for anyone—male or female—to land this gig. Even so, some fresh new voices do find their way onto the big screen to voice movie trailers. "To get a 'new talent' heard," says Vanessa Gilbert of TGMD Talent Agency, "we call up prospective buyers at trailer houses. Sometimes you get them on the phone, sometimes you leave a message, but most of the time you e-mail a small sound bite of something really worthy, attention-getting. What's needed to break into trailers? Talent. Persistence. Desire. Stamina. Humor. Self-promotion."

The read necessary for this type of work is specific to the piece. The role of the voice is to underscore the story of the film. This is not an easy task. You might compare the art of reading trailer copy to painting with a fine sable brush. Each stroke must be perfect so that the depth and color throughout remain smooth and consistent. The voice-over talent must caress each word gently, without sounding like he or she is selling anything, and allow the viewer/listener to hover in a moment in time. Hence the opening line for so many trailers is, "In a world. . . . "

That often-heard line brings to mind the master, the reluctant leader of the trailer voices, Don LaFontaine. Don's career began as a recording engineer in 1965. His career path was forever altered the day a scheduling mix-up occurred and Don's scratch vocal made it to the head of Metro-Goldwyn-Mayer, who was looking for someone to fill in. Don then became the head of trailer production for Kaleidoscope and later Paramount. In 1981, he left New York for Los Angeles and went into business as a freelance voice-over artist. Agent Steve Tisherman began to represent Don, whose voice-over career shows no sign of fading. Don has been involved with the promotion of more than five thousand films to date.

No one voice does all aspects of a trailer campaign. "Coming this summer," "coming soon," "now playing," and all the way to "now on DVD" are done by at least five different voices, each handling a specific part of the launch and promotion of the film.

MARICE TOBIAS, THE VOICE WHISPERER

When you find out where many of these voices are coming from, one woman's name comes up again and again.

Marice Tobias is a master coach. She is different from any other voice-over coach in that she prefers working with only established, professional voice-over talent. In her early years of coaching, Marice was known as the "Voice Shrink," and you would call her if you hit a booking slump. Along the way, she has coached some of the top voice-over talents, many of whom are earning the lion's share of their money in trailers. One of Marice's students refers to her as the

"Voice Whisperer" due to her ability to "hear through" the surface of a read and pinpoint what might be keeping someone from playing full-out.

Marice began her career in New York as a motion-picture script supervisor and freelance copywriter on Madison Avenue. As one of the creative heads of Wells Rich Greene/West, she was the first woman to direct commercials and the first woman to receive a Clio Award. After winning the Clio, she opened her own consulting and production company, Tobias Entertainment Group, specializing in voice-over, hosted programming, and entertainment. Returning to production, she directed her first feature film, *Pulsebeat,* for Vestron.

A director associate of the Actors Studio in New York, Marice began training talent at the Studio and continued on the West Coast, while directing commercials. Tobias's clients and alumni have dominated the top tier of voice-overs, especially trailers, since the early 1990s. At Marlon Brando's request, she directed the star in his last role, the voice of Mrs. Sour in the animated film *Big Bug Man.* Brando passed away three weeks after completing recording.

Here's some advice from Marice. You won't find this in any other book!

> Trailers. The platinum round of the Voice-Over Olympics, the very word brings conversations to a screeching halt while someone inevitably lowers his voice and imitates the trailer read, deciding he too could and probably should "be doing trailer."
>
> Probably not. There is a reason why there are only a handful of people in the world doing the work. It is its own world. It is a world where the essence of an entire film is captured in a few words, seducing, enveloping, tantalizing, or amusing us into its realm. The purest form of acting, it is a distillation of intention and focus—dispassionate passion in drama, action, and epics; wry bemusement in comedy; a tender caress in romance and wonder. Even within the ranks of those who have some or quite a lot of trailer work under their belts, it is a game played in

sudden-death overtime. At any time, the game can be over. You can scratch (trailer talk for auditioning) until your vocal cords are ragged, and in the end, the job will go to one of the heavy hitters.

With so much riding on the voice choice and so many opinions (the trailer house, the production company, the releasing corporation, and sometimes the director) coming to bear on the decision, it's a lot easier and safer to go with proven talent than to take a chance on an outsider. Even a successful film often stays in a theater for only a fraction of its run. If it doesn't make its bones in the first weekend, it's taken off life support and replaced with one that will hopefully sell more popcorn.

But, of course, no one is born on the team. Far from it. The road to finally "finishing" on a trailer is long and grueling. Typically, it's takes at least a year for us to get someone ready to roll. And that's for those who are well established, even high on the promo ladder. It's a matter of being able to do the highly stylized read without sounding like a send-up or imitation. Those already established in trailer are available. We don't need another Don [LaFontaine]. We have the original, and he's as good as it gets.

A new voice makes a place for itself when it sounds like it belongs, thus inspiring trust, yet is different enough to justify putting careers on the line. And yes, that's how high the risk is. Then there's the actual recording session, where the read can be micro-managed to paralysis and your ability to sound like it's take one possibly two and a half years into the development of a campaign for an animated film stretches credulity.

So, when you think you're ready to throw your hat in the trailer ring, make sure you are irrefutably awesome, hone your craft for six more months, and then go for it.

Part 2
Selling Yourself

- **The Demo Reel**
- **Marketing**
- **Working with an Agent**

"Your demo reel is the appetizer, and you are the main course. Keep them wanting more."

—Randy Thomas and Peter Rofé

The Demo Reel

- Reels that get jobs
- Four tips for a successful demo
- Commercial, promo, narration, animation, and live-announce demos
- Recording a demo
- A script for an animation demo by Peter Rofé

A demo reel is a CD compilation of work you have accrued or produced for the purpose of demonstrating your skills as a voice talent. Your demo reel is your calling card, your three-dimensional headshot, and your résumé.

Voice actors with successful careers all began in much the same way we did—by creating a demo filled with spots that never aired anywhere except on our reels. As you begin to actually book work, you replace the homemade spots with real spots, each time replacing the weakest spot of the bunch by something that actually aired somewhere.

Just because you have taken a six-week voice-over course does not necessarily mean you are ready to create a demo, though. In fact, you should watch out for instructors who suggest that you should make a demo after your first series of classes. A professional and honest teacher will tell the student when he or she is truly ready to take this important next step, as it can be quite costly. A good demo can cost between $500 and $2,000 to produce, depending how much booth/studio time is necessary to get the right read on each spot. Also, if you remember that you never get a second chance to make a first impression, you will refrain from making your demo too early in the learning phase.

REELS THAT GET YOU JOBS

It's important to remember that for the rest of your career your demo will continue to be a work in progress and your calling card to those who do the hiring. A great demo can comprise all homemade spots (part of the fake-it-till-you-make-it theory) that you create with a director/producer who helps select the best copy for you. Randy still has one homemade spot on her commercial reel because it continues to get her hired! For those of you who have heard it, she will, of course, never reveal which cut that is (wink).

J. J. Adler, of Abrams Artists Agency in New York and Los Angeles, has this advice for someone putting together a voice-over reel.

> An outstanding demo reel doesn't just show how many voices you do or how much you can sound like that movie trailer guy you've been idolizing all these years. It showcases you at your absolute best. Focus on recording pieces you know you're right for, not what you want to be right for. If you have a knack for announcer reads and have one of "those" voices, the demo should reflect that by concentrating on announcer copy. If your strength is character work and banter, then you should focus more on that.

Good places to hear the demos of other voice artists are the websites geared to these professionals, such as voicebank.net. The demo reels that you can download from these sites are in most cases compilation reels from working voice-over artists who represent the industry's highest standards.

The Commercial Demo

The most often produced demo is the commercial reel. A good commercial reel should include several spots edited back-to-back (with no pauses in between) and last no longer than a minute.

Why so short? If you're an agent or casting director and you receive five or six reels a day, there isn't time in your busy schedule to listen to anything longer. But don't take it personally—a singer auditioning for a Broadway show is typically asked to sing sixteen bars of music and nothing more. You don't have to be a casting director to spot talent

Four Tips for a Successful Demo

Putting together a demo? Here are some tips from J. J. Adler, of Abrams Artists Agency:

- Always put your strongest material first. If we don't hear something good in the first fifteen seconds, chances are we won't stick around to hear that big finale.
- If you're putting together a demo reel for commercials, promos, narration, animation, etc., make sure that you make separate tracks for each style. If you blend them all together, it can appear that you aren't sure what you should be doing . . . or if it's a blend that leads off with a commercial piece, and I'm looking for a promo voice, I'm going to move on.
- You should cover the styles of narration that suit you best. Animation reels are a bit more free-form, but again, you should focus on your strongest stuff. If you're better for cartoon animation, then do that. Or if it's "real person" animation, then tend that way. Length isn't so much of an issue, but generally we get a good sense of what you've got going on in a couple of minutes.
- Updates should be done once a year or so, or when a major new addition (a major national network booking or a new and different style) is available. Conversely, I have clients whose three-year-old reels are still representative. Listen to your reel objectively. If what you hear doesn't sound like the kind of stuff you're doing right now, it's time to revamp your reel.

within the first eight bars of music. You might think of it this way: Your demo reel is the appetizer, and *you* are the main course. Keep them wanting more. Therefore, it is very important that you keep your reel short and put your best stuff up front.

"I always think the shorter the better," says Lisa Marber-Rich of Atlas Talent Agency. "People's attention spans have gotten a lot shorter since the fax machine was invented, and I think that a minute is a pretty decent reel. You can always have multiple reels, but I think when you're sending things out, people don't want to listen to more than a minute."

Five spots will sufficiently showcase your range and vocal abilities. Try to exhibit your personality, style, sense of humor, and ability to be taken seriously as an authoritative figure—let each spot showcase one of those qualities. Use only material that you and your coach feel is your strong suit. Pick spots from both radio and television that suit your style and vocal qualities, and use *real* commercial copy—do not write copy on your own! But stay away from celebrity endorsements or highly recognizable voices for certain product lines. Everyone knows James Earl Jones is the voice of Verizon, and yours will seem like a poor imitation in comparison. Find lesser-known spots that could plausibly be your own.

You don't need to do each spot in its entirety. With roughly twelve seconds per spot, you don't have time for that anyway. Your opening spot should start from the beginning, establish itself, then cut away as soon as you've established your read, vocal quality, and point of view. Your second spot can start from the middle and finish to the end. Your third and fourth spots can start from beginning, middle, or end. Your fifth and final spot is your closer. Make sure it puts a "button" on the end of the reel to let the listener know that the reel is over. That's why many reels end on a tagline ("American Express. Don't leave home without it.").

Go for contrast and juxtaposition in the vocal tone, message, and production value of each spot. If you open with a piece that is your strongest full-voice read, then the next spot should be a softer presentation in which the vocal projection is vastly different. This not only gives you a different read but also showcases your ability to work the microphone, giving you a completely different sound. The challenge is simple if you use your imagination and creativity.

The Promo Demo

Promo reels should be similar to commercial reels in that you should put your best stuff first and keep the entire reel to a minute in length. A promo demo needs to be a quick and seamless succession of highly produced, current-sounding promos, complete with the SOT (sound on tape) excerpts from the show or shows you are promoting. Promo material comes from the news ("Should a doctor be allowed to help a patient die? Final choices, tonight on *NBC Nightly News*"), sitcoms, dramas, game shows, concerts, and more. Promos are all very much the same in that they promote a time-sensitive event. But reads may vary tremendously given the target audience and the event being promoted, so make sure your reel has the variety it needs. The more time you spend researching different types of programming, the more variety your reel will have.

When you choose a producer for your promo demo, that person should specialize in producing and creating competitive and creative demos for this field. Someone who is a good commercial demo producer is not necessarily a good judge of promo content, sound, and style.

The Narration Demo

For your narration demo you want something you'll be able to sink your teeth into, so choose material that speaks to you and interests you. Again, five spots seem to demonstrate enough versatility without boring your audience. A narration reel should include text from a variety of programming such as you'd find on the Discovery Channel, Court TV, the Learning Channel, Nova, Home & Garden, and Animal Planet. It may also include medical narrations (instructional videos for doctors and medical students), corporate industrials (in-house employee training videos, trade show presentations), acoustic guide tours for museums, and educational narrations (standardized test prompts). Putting narrations from a variety of genres on your reel will showcase your range and marketability. Unlike what you'd do with a commercial reel, on a narration reel you will want to sustain the read, so your reel can be a bit longer, but it should never exceed two minutes in length.

The Animation Demo

In an animation demo, variety in vocal qualities and characters, as well as original and entertaining material, will keep the listener engaged.

The first step is to make a list of all the character voices you think are inside you—these can be originals or imitations of existing characters (see page 71 to 73 for some suggestions). If you don't do a perfect impersonation of a preexisting character, do not put it on your demo reel. Also, create your own copy—material from existing cartoons or animated feature films will do you a disservice and come across as a poor man's version of what the original was, and you won't get to showcase your own natural abilities and creativity.

An original script written around your characters should create a loosely based timeline that cleverly ties all of your characters together, keeping the listener engaged and curious to hear how the story pans out.

The Live Announce Demo

The advent of TiVO has made researching award and game shows as simple as clicking a few buttons. Record as many award and game shows as possible, then sit with a pen and paper, and write out the opening segments for any type of show you want to include on your demo. Then choose the appropriate style of music to accompany the opening, along with an applause track.

> "Above all, have fun. You are embarking on a career that can potentially pay you hundreds of thousands of dollars or more to say things you got in trouble for as a kid!"
>
> —Marc Graue, demo producer

Have fun with your read and feel free to take it over the top so that you can recreate the energy of being in a live venue with all of the excitement only a live audience can bring. As you'll hear when you listen to the awards shows, the announcer's voice should be full-bodied and projected, so it can be heard above the cacophony of music, applause, and shrieks of young audience members, such as you will find at the Nickelodeon Kids' Choice Awards. With the proper pacing and production elements, you are good to go!

RECORDING THE DEMO

Before you record your demo, make sure that you have a clear vision of what you do best and how you can present your best effort before you begin. Be prepared to spend the money necessary to guarantee that your demo will be the best it can be. That might mean using a studio and a good producer. Toward that end, many voice artists have turned to Marc Graue. Marc is the owner of Marc Graue Recording Studios in Burbank, California. Almost every major agency sends talent to Marc because, to put it simply, no one on the West Coast does a better job. We asked Marc for some words of wisdom from his experience working with some of the best talent around:

> Make sure when that whoever is producing your demo knows the voice-over biz. Get your copy (script) ahead of time so you know what you'll be recording. Make sure you are working with someone who has actually directed voice-over sessions before. Be comfortable. This is your demo, so make sure that the studio will accommodate your needs. Don't be embarrassed. "I really need a bedroom voice on this spot like you've just finished making love . . ." is direction to get a great read from you, not a request for services! Above all, have fun. You are embarking on a career that can potentially pay you hundreds of thousands of dollars or more to say things you got in trouble for as a kid!

You will record your demo either in a professional studio or in your home studio. (Unless you are in one of the major markets—New York, Los Angeles, or Chicago—you cannot compete in voice-over unless you have a home studio; see chapter 14 for more about setting one up.) If you're recording from home, you can find a director who can work with you over the phone.

Once you have created enough perfect takes, you can send the audio to a top producer who specializes in that category of voice-over (promo, animation, etc.) who will put all the bells and whistles on it and send it back to you as a finalized MP3 file.

Finally, remember: A demo is *only as good as its ability to hold the attention of the people who are listening to it.* The more you hold their attention, the more likely they are to remember you when casting their next job.

A SCRIPT BY PETER

To help one of my clients, Jen Cohn, write a script for an animation demo, we worked together to discover what characters Jen had the ability to create, modify, and imitate. During the process, we spent a lot of time laughing with a purpose: to see exactly what Jen could do with her mouth and her mind. For the reel, we chose the most diverse characters Jen offered, from a physical, vocal, and mental point of view. We also carefully chose characters for the demo. They had to be just right because there is a time constraint; an animation demo should never be longer than two minutes. This "teaser" format allows you to showcase only the best of what you can do, leaving the listener thinking that you have much more to offer—and providing the impetus for producers and casting directors to call you in and have you read in person.

We chose characters from a variety of different locales, age ranges, races, genders, religions, and intelligence levels. The story line of the script gave us the flexibility to open with Jen in her own voice, presenting her own faux riches-to-rags-to-riches story as it would appear on National Public Radio's *This American Life,* a popular contemporary radio show. Listeners are already prepared for what is to follow, and by now, their curiosity is piqued. Note that Jen's name is mentioned several times throughout the reel. This was an intentional effort to plant a subliminal seed in the mind of the listener: "Jen Cohn . . . where have I heard that name before?"

We noted cues in the script so the engineer could add music and sound effects to the vocal tracking, adding authenticity to the reel.

Jen Cohn's Animation Reel

Music: NPR Starter Music
NPR HOST: Tonight on This American Life we bring you a story of tragedy and triumph. The rise, fall, and inflections of voice artist . . . Jen Cohn.

SFX (sound effects): city street
Upper West Sider: I was a sophomore at Barnard when I gave birth to Jen and there was no way I could keep her. So while I was on a layover in Mississippi on the way to Boca I left her at a church doorstep.

Music: Gospel Music

Mama: I done found Jenny in that little pink blanket. She was the sweetest thing (oh she was). And I took her in as one of my own.

Papa: For as long as we could remember that child would open her mouth and make the funniest voices you ever did hear, hmmm . . . mmm. We all knew she make good somehow.

SFX: school ambience

Gita: Jen Cohn was a scholarship student at Miss Elsie's back when I was dean. She dressed like a ragamuffin and needed her nose done, but, darling, she was sharp. Sharp as a tack.

Music: Edith Piaf

Yvette: When she came to Paris she did not know the first thing about which fork to use, or what scarf goes with what skirt. How to pronounce the word "pffff." I had to teach her everything.

Music: techno runway music

Sophia: I met her backstage at the collections in Milan. She was busy shaving Donatella's back, and I said, "Cara mia, this is no way for a girl with your voice to make a living."

Music: "Imagine"

Yoko Ono: Plastic Ono Band was scheduled for a show at CBGB, and I was busy working on "Imagine" with John, so Jen came in as a last-minute replacement.

John Lennon: Jen changed rock 'n' roll forever, man. She was a star before she hit the stage.

Music: rock 'n' roll (Motley Crue)

Pamela Anderson: Tommy introduced us after her show at the Hollywood Bowl. She was fucking cool. The things she taught me to do with the microphone. Well, you saw the video.

Deborah Schwartz: We all knew she had demons. I mean how could you do what she was doing on stage otherwise, right? I think that all the money and adulation just got to her.

Rosie Perez: That's when I staged the intervention. And we found out that she was like hooked . . . hooked on phonics. She was shooting up like four or five words a day. It was disgusting.

SFX: traffic, car pulling up, limo window rolls down, car door opens and closes

Kathleen Turner: Jen was standing off the Cross Bronx Expressway when I spotted her. A common voice hooker. When she saw me through the limousine window she cried, "Kathleen, please help me!" Having been vocally confused myself, I opened the door and hurried her in.

Music: Klezmer

Rabbi Schmulle: She needed faith. She needed to find respect, respect for her instrument. I told her with a strict regimen of torah, tsedaka, and a glass of hot water with lemon she would be back in the booth in no time!

NPR HOST: And so she did. Jen came back with a vengeance. Countless commercials, cartoons, and campaigns later, Jen Cohn is back on vocal track.

SFX: radio station changes

Sancho: That show was really informative.

Charlie: I'll say. She's a real tour de force.

Dumb Guy: Huh . . . I didn't know she rode bicycles.

Jen: Okay, guys, that's enough. I think they get the picture. If they want to hear more of me, they can call. Meanwhile, we got a booking to get to. Later.

[Litany of good-byes from a variety of Jen's characters]

Marketing

10

- Packaging your demo
- Designing the package
- Writing a cover letter
- Follow-up postcards and e-mails
- Technology and marketing

Okay, you now have a fully produced demo reel that showcases your ability to do the work. Whether the demo reel is geared toward commercials, promos, narration, animation, or all of the above, the next and crucial step is marketing.

PACKAGING YOUR DEMO

You will want to put together a package in which to mail your demo reel to prospective clients. The essential elements of this CD package are:

- CD
- CD cover
- CD tray card with spine
- CD label
- Business card
- Cover letter, on personalized stationery
- Postcard, for follow-ups

Since you have spent a good deal of time and money honing your craft and producing your reel(s), spend the extra time and money it takes for this demo reel package to look good, too. All your marketing materials should have a uniform design, keeping your package consistent and memorable. Your contact information should be displayed on

With a Little Help from Your Friends

Before you mail any of your CDs to the industry, here's something that you can do directly and inexpensively from your home and that may yield quick results. Why not send an e-mail letter and an MP3 attachment of your reel to everyone in your e-mail address book? Include your business contacts, friends, and family, and send a note like this:

> Dear Friends, Family, and Colleagues:
>
> As some of you know, I have been pursuing a career in voice-overs. I have attached my demo reel to this e-mail in MP3 format so that you can download it in seconds and listen on your home or office computer. If you know anybody in this industry (or not) who could help me get voice-over work, please forward my reel to them. It would be greatly appreciated. I hope you enjoy the reel and I look forward to hearing back from you.

This quick e-mail can make a world of difference. Many folks who are not familiar with the voice-over industry will find your demo fascinating, and opportunities may be uncovered in the most unlikely of places. At a wedding reception, Peter was seated at a table next to a woman he'd never met. "After telling her I was a professional voice-over artist, I gave her my business card and suggested that I e-mail her my reel. She passed it on to her cousin, an executive in children's programming. He heard it and played it for his department, who decided that I was the perfect voice for their new ad campaign."

all materials, making it utterly impossible for someone to be unable to find you. Here are some essential aspects that you will need to pay attention to:

• Your name should be displayed prominently.

• Your contact information, starting with your primary phone number, should appear beneath your name.

• Include a cell-phone number in the event that the casting house or agent has trouble reaching you at your primary number—you certainly wouldn't want to miss out on any opportunities.

- An e-mail address is always helpful. If you have a website with down-loadable files of your demo reels, include its address as well.
- Display any union affiliations on the CD cover.
- It is important to package your CD in a thick jewel case so you can put your name and phone number or other contact information on the spine. This will allow your contact to locate your reel easily on a shelf.

Graphic Design

Agents, casting directors, producers, and creative directors are likely to make snap judgments the moment they open your mailing envelope. Within that split second, you want to make a positive and long-lasting impression. Therefore, it is essential that the design of your package exemplify who you are as a voice artist in a professional manner. For instance, if you have a voice that carries distinction and authority, your CD cover should reflect that with strong, clean type and bold colors. If you're an animation artist, you may want to use cartoon-like graphics to demonstrate what's in the package.

All of the materials you send out—CD cover, label, business card, stationery, and postcard—should have a consistent design. It's well worth your money to hire a graphic designer whose work is creative and professional. Voice announcers who work make a very good living, and many of them spend quite a bit on the way their packages look—you want your materials to look like you spent some money on them, too. Think of the expenditure as investing in a business. You are, after all, opening your own business, and that requires a professionally designed business card, stationery, and logo.

We have two caveats about graphic design. One, we don't believe in putting a photograph of the artist on the reel. If you do, you might be typecast based on physical appearance alone. The other cautionary note is to make sure the design sparks an interest in you without over-shadowing what you demonstrate on the CD. Less is more. Likewise, the image or corporate logo you choose should not overshadow your name and contact information. That's why we believe keeping it simple with clean lines and a few choice colors to do the job.

The Cover Letter

Your package should include a clean, succinct cover letter that clearly states who you are and what you do. Your cover letter may vary slightly depending upon who you're sending it to, but here's a basic template:

Dear Josh,

I've enclosed a copy of my one-minute commercial reel for your consideration. I have studied voice-over technique with Peter Rofé for the last six months. I am a working voice-over artist in the New York metropolitan area specializing in fun, hip, edgy, "real guy" commercial reads. I trust you will keep my reel on file for future reference, as I am readily available for auditions and bookings.

I look forward to working with you in the future.

Sincerely,
Rick Lawson

We suggest you limit your mailings to ten leads a week. This makes the task much less arduous and makes it easy to keep on top of the leads to whom you send your demo reel—who they are, where they work, and what they do. You will be better acquainted with your possible contacts and able to recognize someone who calls you with work. Doing incremental mailings also gives you the opportunity to keep your cover letter up-to-date to reflect your latest voice-over work. Any time you do a job, change your cover letter accordingly.

Follow-up Postcards and E-mails

Let's assume you've sent out ten reels this week. Two months from today, you are ready to embark on the follow-up process, which includes sending a postcard. The design of the postcard clearly resembles that of your CD cover and will remind the recipient to listen to your CD or to get in touch with you if they have listened and liked what they heard but have simply dropped the ball and not called you. You are reminding your leads that even if they have forgotten about you, you haven't forgotten about them.

Postcards are great follow-up devices because the addressee doesn't have to open an envelope or spend more than a few seconds reading it. This time, your salutation is hand-written in a more casual, conversational approach. For instance:

> Hey, Josh,
>
> Back in August, I sent you a copy of my one-minute commercial reel. In the event that you did not receive it, please e-mail me at rick@ricklawson.com or call me at 555-123-4567 and I will send an e-mail with my demo reel attached. I look forward to hearing back from you.
>
> Rick

Give the recipient a month. If you haven't heard, send a personalized e-mail and a link to your demo recording. (Don't send an mp3 file without asking permission first, as you don't want to clog the recipient's mailbox.) If you don't have an e-mail address, call the company and get one from a receptionist, or check the company website—do not speak to the lead directly.

> Dear Josh,
>
> Back in August, I mailed you a hard cover copy of my one-minute commercial voice-over reel. I followed up with a postcard a few months later and I have yet to hear back from you. I am now e-mailing you this link to my demo to ensure that you will receive it and have the opportunity to listen to it at your earliest convenience. Thank you so much for taking the time. I look forward to meeting you someday.
>
> Sincerely,
> Rick Lawson

Once you have completed this three-part process of initial mailing, postcard follow-up, and e-mail reminder, you have exhausted all your options. By no means should you try to reach this person again, but you should continue to reach out to other leads. Countless folks learn the voice-over craft, but it's those who don't let rejection and lack of response get them down and who continue to mail out reels each and every week for years who survive in our competitive industry. You do not need all of these leads to like you, love you, or even to reach out to you. All you need is one lead to show interest. That alone may be the beginning of a voice-over career.

TECHNOLOGY AND MARKETING

You should create a website that includes your demos and reflects who you are through its look and feel—that is, the design, images, and type faces, as well as your logo and examples of your work, will all create an image of who you are. Your main goal, of course, is to come across as a dedicated professional. Your website is your calling card. Let it reflect you and your voice in the very best light!

Dozens of online marketing companies now allow you to showcase your demo. Two websites have proven to be especially valuable resources for producers, casting directors, advertising agencies, animation houses, recording facilities, and, of course, voice-over artists. Voice123.com and voices.com serve as voice-over search engines and online voiceover marketplaces. On their sites producers can listen to voice-over reels and find artists who suit their needs, and they allow voice-over artists to record and submit auditions directly to producers via the Internet. Among their many advantages, these services:

- Broaden the market for voice artists, by making their demo reels available online for thousands of ad agencies, producers, and other clients to hear;
- Provide the means to audition online, which streamlines the audition process for clients, who can choose the number of auditions they would like to receive, and from which types of voices, gender, et cetera; and
- Provide a wealth of resources for the voice artist, including scripts, blogs, tips and advice, business news, tutorials, and other information.

Working with an Agent

11

- Getting an agent
- What to do once you have an agent
- Investing in your career
- Keeping the agent-client relationship alive
- Randy's agency story

When you think of a talent agent, do you picture a slick-talking, Hollywood agent like Jeremy Piven's character Ari Gold in the HBO series Entourage? Or does Woody Allen's stereotypical, fast-talking New York agent Broadway Danny Rose come to mind?

Agents come in all shapes and sizes, and "the art of agent-ing" is not a one-size-fits-all business.

Finding the right agent can be one of your most important career moves. Once you are on the road to success at voice-over, a good agent can help you navigate the often slippery slope to success as a voice actor. Having the right agent gives you more quality job opportunities than you would likely unearth on your own. Buyers/clients will respect you because they know your agent is looking out for your best interests by negotiating and nailing down the deal before you walk through the door to do the job. Having the business part taken care of by a capable professional, you can walk into a recording session as a voice for hire "ready to throw it down" (slang for do a great job).

HOW DO YOU GET AN AGENT?

As your career progresses, at some point you will be ready for representation, but to get an agent interested, you first have to show you have the talent and resources (training, perseverance, flexibility) to succeed in this business.

The first step in this process is to join an online voice-over marketplace (see "Technology and Marketing," in chapter 10) and try to consistently get bookings. These jobs can be small at first, but, perhaps surprisingly, large national and regional accounts can also be booked though online companies. Once you have a national or regional campaign under your belt, make sure that spot is on your reel. You should also reference that booking in the first paragraph of the letter you send to any prospective agent.

The next step is to find an agency that will be right for you. While the biggest agencies have no reason to take on unproven talent, plenty of agencies will take a chance on a newbie. Even as a newbie, however, never approach an agent until you have something to present that displays your depth of talent, discipline, and commitment to the craft.

Find the agency you want to approach, learn all you can about that agency, then write a great letter. We can't emphasize enough how helpful it is, in the first paragraph of your letter, to mention the name of a reference who knows one of the agents in the agency as well as the national and regional work you have done.

The website www.voicebank.net hosts many voice-over talent agencies in the United States and Canada, lists the top people they represent, and lets you download demos of these artists. It would behoove you to listen to every man or woman in your category and even mention a particular actor to whom you sound similar when you write your letter to an agency. It's also a plus if you are very different from anyone a given agency represents and can offer something new. Better yet, find a well-known voice-over artist from a competing agency with whom you can compare your sound or delivery. This can be particularly effective if you know that person is getting a lot of work.

Do you have good news to share, like landing a national gig? It may be your entrée to an agency. For example, a young, up-and-coming voice for hire we know booked a national spot to air during the Super Bowl through an online voice-over marketplace. To announce timely news like this, send out a postcard or an e-mail that is short, concise, and clever.

If you are presenting your demo to an agent for the first time, you should mail it to the agency, where it will most likely be placed in a stack with all the other unsolicited demos. And don't lose heart: Almost every agent we know takes the time to listen to demos and weeds out the wheat from the chaff or at least has an assistant do so. Most agents set aside time to look at a fresh pool of talent. That can be the end of the calendar year, after tax season, or during the summer. A handful of demos may make it to the meeting where agents discuss new signings or talent they are interested in looking at—and with persistence that will be you.

OMG, I HAVE AN AGENT!

When you get that call or e-mail from an agent letting you know you are being considered, be ready for an audition on the spot. The agency may fax or e-mail you various types of copy and ask you to either read cold on the phone or to record your reading and send them your "audition."

Before you sign a contract, make sure the agency is reputable. Have you been asked to pay a fee to join the agency? If so, this is not a legitimate agency. Is there a fee to appear on the agency website? This alone does not mean the agency is disreputable, but it does mean that the website is "for sale," and you may want to question the caliber of buyers who are willing to pay for talent who can purchase representation this way. If you have been asked to pay more than 10 percent of your fee as a commission, this is *not* a legitimate franchised and licensed agency. It's important, too, that you get a good feeling about joining the agency. Your agent should be as excited about having you as a client as you are to have an agent.

This honeymoon phase with an agent doesn't last long, about the length of one lunar cycle if you're lucky.

A new agency will generally ask you to audition for everything to determine the range and scope of your talents and abilities. Many agencies distribute forms that list every type of read found in casting breakdowns. You can check off as many different types of reads as you can do in order to indicate exactly what kinds of commercials or projects are in your range.

Your versatility will give your new agent a chance to know exactly what your strengths are. Eventually the agency will have an understanding of what you can do and from then on will bring you in only for the things you are right for you, the gigs the agency believes you have a shot at booking.

Before actually signing you, an agent is very likely to establish a trial period of three, six, or twelve months. An agency may not actually sign you but will be happy to let you use their name and promote yourself as if you were actually signed. This is a win-win deal. You and the agency can give each other a test drive around the block, so to speak, and you are able to decide if this is the right agency for you.

It is not unusual for a voice artist to have several agents. You can sign with agencies in Dallas, Atlanta, and San Francisco, giving them exclusive rights in their respective markets, and also sign with major agencies in New York or Los Angeles and book national work through them. Obviously, it's easier to get an agent in Dallas or Atlanta than it is to sign with one in New York or Los Angeles. Start small and work your way up, knowing that you will be more experienced and ready to handle success when you get to a New York, Chicago, or Los Angeles talent agency.

Once your agent begins getting you auditions, you're off and running. This is the beginning of all the exciting things that can happen for someone who takes this craft to heart and gives it their all.

INVESTING IN YOUR CAREER

Once you sign with an agent—whether it is your first time being signed to an agency or you're a seasoned professional moving to a new agent—there is a short-lived honeymoon period. This phase with an agent doesn't last long, about the length of one lunar cycle if you're lucky. Booking work is the best way to get your new agent's attention and keep it, and for this reason we suggest you wait to get an agent until you are ready to consistently hit the ball out of the park with your auditions.

In the 1990s, upon signing with an agency, a voice artist would typically request that the agency mail a demo to advertising agencies, casting directors, and other carefully selected buyers, to get the word out that the agency was representing a new talent. Most agencies were willing to do this, provided the talent paid for the postage, mailing envelopes, and any other ancillary costs. The cost would be somewhere between $500 and $1,000, or more.

Today we would recommend that you spend this money instead on the marketing efforts we discuss in chapter 10. Choosing to spend money in these areas of self-marketing and promotion lets your agent know that you are making a strong commitment toward your career, so he or she may work more diligently on your behalf in support of that effort. Continue to take acting classes, as well as private voice-over sessions with master coaches, and let your agent know you are doing so. Your go-getter attitude will definitely resonate with your agent.

If you feel the agency is not making a responsible effort to promote you alongside its other talent, the best option is to make a change.

Making the choice to invest in your career may pay off in short order, or it may take longer to see a true return on your investment. With the number of talented candidates out there, competition is always fierce, so you need to do whatever you can afford to gain an edge. The fact you are so committed to the goal of being successful is worthy of a big pat on the back. Congratulations! You are now playing with the "big dogs."

REKINDLING THE SPARK . . . OR REVIVING A DEAD SHARK

Your relationship with your agent may bring to mind Woody Allen's observation in *Annie Hall*: "A relationship is like a shark. It has to keep moving to stay alive. What we have here is a dead shark." So, let's say you have an agent and you are booking an occasional spot or two, but you are not even listed on the agency website and you feel you are not getting the quality of attention you deserve. Or, maybe it's just a question of your agent not being able to imagine you doing a certain type of voice work or spots you'd like to be doing. What can you do? Jump up and down and make a fuss, or stay put and quietly sulk and speak badly about your agency to anyone who will listen?

If you feel the agency is not making a reasonable effort to promote you alongside its other talent, the best option is to make a change. Check the expiration date of your current contract, then make discreet inquiries to other agencies to see if there will be interest in your talents when you become eligible to sign with a new agent who has your best interests at heart. Two things to keep in mind. One, do *not* leave an agent until you have locked in new representation. Two, make sure a new agent can promote or sell you with passion and without fear they will be undercutting their other clients (sometimes a new client can create a conflict of interest with other clients, and you don't want to work with an agent who has such constraints).

You and your agent will be working in unison to move your career forward, but you are the one who does the work and is responsible for promoting your career. So take your responsibilities to heart and do everything you can to be the best you can be. Then trust that the universe (and your agent) can bring you great opportunities.

RANDY'S AGENCY STORY

I found my first agent in 1992. I targeted an agency and made numerous calls to the agency, only to be rebuffed by the assistant agent, who told me, in not-so-nice words, that they had a full client roster and I need not call again.

I soon found a client who wanted to hire me for a voice-over. I spoke with that same assistant agent again and said, "Look, I have clients calling me all the time for bookings. I just want an agency to put them through and book the work." Needless to say, that got the assistant agent's attention, and the following week I was sitting in the main agent's office, signing a contract.

My twenty-year broadcasting career as a radio DJ taught me how to be professional and cool under fire, and to work a microphone. Even though the art of voice-over was unknown territory, my confidence gave me the ability to make people feel at ease around me. New agents who are considering signing you need to feel they are making the right choice, and interacting with someone who shows a lot of self-confidence (but not bravado) makes the decision process much easier for them.

Once I could finally say I had an agent, I came to some conclusions. I knew this agency was not getting a huge number of auditions coming through the office. I felt I would have a better chance of winning more auditions and booking more commercials if I were at an agency that had more clout and was getting more calls for actors to audition. So, I moved up a few rungs on the ladder of talent agencies in Los Angeles. I continued to book some commercials as well as the live broadcasts and television shows. After a short time I realized that I was not connecting with any one agent in that office, so I moved on to the agency of my dreams. I had worked hard at my craft. I had taken all the necessary classes and worked enough to gain entrée to this great and renowned agency. I felt I deserved to be at this top agency, where auditions were so plentiful that I began booking like crazy.

Around this time my husband, Arnie Wohl, who acts as my manager, noticed that there was a lot of work in the field of promotional spots (promos) and radio imaging. "Promo/affiliate/radio and narration" is a specific type of work, and a specialized niche group of voice-over artists doing it were at that time being booked by a small group of agents in New York. I made the decision to seek representation with a New York agent who was busy working in this radio and affiliate promo business, along with certain "New York only" commercials. Having a New York agent would mean more work and more money, and I could promote the part of my career that L.A. agents were either uninformed about or not interested in. Since I was living and working in Hollywood's voice-over community, a Los Angeles agent was also a necessity.

Having jumped on the bicoastal representation bandwagon before most other voice artists, I was soon booking radio station promos along with a few television affiliate promos across America. They were seeing and hearing the potential of the female voice. Being seen and heard as an innovator for women in this field was one of the inspirations for my marketing slogan at the time, "Sometimes the Best Man for the Job Is a Woman."

I have since signed with two other agents, only to have finally returned to Atlas Talent Agency in New York, and with Tisherman, Gilbert, Motley and Drozdoski (TGMD) in Los Angeles. For me and what I do best—radio, television, and live announcing—Atlas Talent is perfect, and TGMD is ideal for promo work and trailers. As the branding voice of *Entertainment Tonight* and *The Insider* for several years, I worked alongside Don LaFontaine, who is also represented by TGMD. In fact, Don has been with the agency since he first signed with Steve Tisherman back in the 1980s. When Steve decided to pass the torch along to his agents, he very generously created TGMD.

So, while I moved around trying out various agencies in search of the perfect fit, Don has been loyal to his first agent. Don's relationship has helped to build both his career and that of TGMD, and they are both enjoying the benefits of all they've accomplished together.

Part 3
The Working Voice Artist

- **Auditions**
- **Bookings**
- **Home Studios and Technology**
- **More Advice from the Pros**

"If you don't believe it, don't expect anybody else to. Honesty—if you can fake that, you've got it made."

—Don LaFontaine, famous promo announcer

Auditions

12

- How auditions work
- Where you'll audition
- Audition advice from the pros
- The art of auditioning

Okay, you've landed an audition. Great. This is your chance to book a spot that will pay you money, advance your career, and give you the confidence to build upon your success and move your career a few steps beyond where you were last week. This is the playing field where you have the opportunity to run a touchdown and get a great job.

Keep in mind, first and foremost, that you should treat every audition with the same respect you show for every job you do (remember, without auditions there would be no jobs!), and you must remain focused on doing the best you can. The successful actors you are reading against are focused on what they are doing, and they want to take that job opportunity away from you and book it for themselves.

An audition presents you with a few fleeting moments to showcase your abilities, so make the most of those moments by taking time in advance to prepare. Break down a script, analyze the copywriter's objective, rehearse your part out loud. Lack of preparation often leads to a mediocre read, while preparing for an audition and giving a great read can, in fact, be the sole factor in making or breaking a voice-over career.

No one can definitively state how to win consistently at auditions, because every audition is different. Statistically, if you book one job for every fifty auditions you have a pretty good batting average. The one overriding truth is that you must remain undaunted and give it your best every time you stand in front of a microphone.

RULES OF THE GAME

It is your agent's responsibility to give you the background information you need before you arrive at your audition—the call time for the audition, the product or service you will be reading for, the role you will be playing, and the spot's intended recording date. Pay special attention

---

Audition Advice from Randy and Others

I used to be intimidated by the caliber of actors who were signing in to read for the same spot I was there to read for. I would defeat myself before I ever got behind the microphone. That was until the day I was number fifty-one out of one hundred actors who auditioned. The ad agency told me they listened to every woman who read, as well as the men, and I was the one they chose. I realized at that moment that there is only one me and I am the best me in the world. The lesson I learned is how important it is to trust in the knowledge that no one else is like you. What you bring to the read is what makes you special, so zero in on what makes you special and read the copy as though you are the only one that should be reading it. Nobody can be a better *you*.

Here are some insights from other professionals who audition consistently and consistently well:

Find all your voices before you try to find work. Versatility will get you more business and prevent you from being put into a "box" as a one-note player.

Read, read, read. Everything and anything. Recite the words to your favorite songs. Recite the Pledge of Allegiance. Recite the words at the base of the Statue of Liberty. Bring tears to your own eyes.

Believe what you are reading for a client. If you don't believe it, don't expect anybody else to. Honesty—if you can fake that, you've got it made.

—Don LaFontaine

When someone asks what you do for a living, proudly respond, "I audition."

Being a V.O. actor is a lot like being an athlete. Never go into an audition or gig without being well prepared and properly warmed-up. Your agent

to this last point. Let your agent know if you will not be available on the scheduled date. You definitely don't want to be in the position of not being able to show up and record a spot for which you've been booked.

---

gets you the audition, books your gigs, and makes sure you get paid. *You* promote your career.

—Mark Avery

My father, Bill McCord, was an NBC staff announcer in New York for thirty years. When I expanded into voice-over, he gave me the following advice: Show up on time; work quickly; have no opinions; don't give anybody any crap.

In the more than ten years that I've been doing voice-overs, this is the only advice that has ever mattered, although I might add one more thing an actress told me when I started going out: "Do your best in your audition, then go home and don't think about it again. Anything anybody else tells you is a bunch of s**t."

—Billy Vera

Auditions? Unless they specifically asked for you (or your style), go in with confidence but assume you're not going to get the gig—that way you have nothing to lose.

Give them what they ask for, then, if time allows, give them something they didn't expect. Once again, let it all hang out. You might surprise them—hey, you might surprise yourself.

—Michael Sheehy

Once you get into the game, it's very much a matter of the buyer's taste. Just about everyone in that audition room is very good at what they do and could do the job. It's just a matter of what they're in the mood for that day. Do they want a kiwi or a tangelo?

—Jennifer Hale

Here are some other things to keep in mind:

- Leave yourself ample time to travel to your audition in a relaxed fashion. Nothing is worse than arriving late or feeling stressed out by a difficult commute. Plan to arrive at your audition thirty minutes before your call time. Not only will you avoid the stress of worrying about being late; you'll also be able to devote some last-minute and perhaps invaluable time to reading your script again and refining your approach to it.

- The first thing to do after signing in is to identify and confirm the role you have been submitted for and that you have the correct copy. In many cases, several casting sessions will be held simultaneously at the same audition facility and the scene can be confusing.

- Find a comfortable place where you can read your copy without distractions. This is sometimes easier said than done. Many voice actors turn their auditions into social gatherings. It's fun to see colleagues and friends on the audition circuit, but some actors enjoy this camaraderie at the expense of other actors in the waiting room who are trying to concentrate on their scripts and compete for work. If this happens to you, a bathroom, corridor, or stairway can provide the perfect hideaway where you can prepare for your audition in peace and quiet.

WHERE YOU'LL AUDITION

Many national commercial auditions are held at a casting director's office, or at the talent representative's office, in their in-house voice-over booths. The larger talent agencies, such as CESD, Buchwald, Atlas, and Abrams, also hold many auditions in-house, while an independent casting director will use audition facilities in various locations around a city. An ad agency that represents the commercial client might also host auditions, using in-house recording facilities. The talent agencies usually have a skilled agent and/or assistant who records and coaches the talent toward what they believe is a more competitive read. A casting director might also critique the artist's first or second reads, although this casting director has no allegiance to the artists reading.

These days, when so many professional voice-over artists have the ability to do almost all of their work digitally, agents also send out audition scripts to their talent who have recording studios in their homes. If you have the luxury to record, edit, and upload or e-mail your audio, you can do anything you choose. Read the copy a few times, listen, stop, and record it again, honing and polishing the read a little at a time. You can go back and just do a pick up (re-read) on the lines you thought could be better, and then edit them in seamlessly. You can continue this process until you are completely happy with your read. The next step is to send in your audition via the Internet.

Wherever you audition, the most important thing you need to concern yourself with is bringing your best read, or performance, to the copy. It's not uncommon for a director to tell you to do your read one way, but all the while a little internal voice in your head might be saying, "I think it should be read differently." When this happens—and it will!—don't walk away from the microphone without asking for one more take. Of course, your assignment is to make the person who is directing you happy with your performance, but pay attention to the "little voice," too. Now that the pressure of pleasing the director is lifted, you have a chance to wow with your own special zing.

THE ART OF AUDITIONING

Sound Lounge Radio creative director Tony Mennuto is an expert on the art of voice-over auditioning. Sound Lounge is one of the largest voice-over production facilities in the country, and Tony has auditioned thousands of voice artists for the majority of today's national radio and TV commercials Sound Lounge produces. His previous experience—ad-agency copywriter, voice-over actor, television producer—also gives him a unique and complete perspective on the voice-over business.

What do you look for in talent at an audition?
One, a good actor. I honestly believe that a great voice is only about 30 percent of a successful voice-over audition. I find that good actors can often perform a commercial script and make it come to life. They take the time to prepare their reads using acting techniques, and perform it—almost like a mini-scene from a play or film.

Two, someone who is easy to work with. I often think beyond the audition, because if the actor books the job, chances are I will have to be in the recording session with him when we actually record the commercial. There I will also need to feel good about introducing him to my client (who is paying around $400 an hour for studio time). "Professional," "on time," and "ready to go when it's his turn" also go under this heading.

> "I honestly believe that a great voice is only about 30 percent of a successful voice-over audition."
> —Tony Mennuto, creative director, Sound Lounge Radio

Three, someone who can take direction. Prior to the casting session, I have discussed the commercial with the copywriter, who lets me know exactly what type of read they are going for (ironic, excited, etc.). The talent needs to be able to take this direction. However, that is not to say that I don't encourage talent to try his or her own interpretation of the script. Sometimes, that's where the most natural, interesting reads come from.

How do you work with the talent?
As a former voice-over person, I know that the audition can be a stressful experience. I like to keep things light (and hopefully fun) in order to encourage a great performance. It's important to remember that a good casting session also makes me look good, so I'm out to get the best performances possible.

In terms of voice quality and potential, the good news is that there is a market for all kinds of voices out there. Some commercials need "regular" sounding people, some need "news announcer" types—what matters most is performance. The bad news is that you never know what's going to be in style at the time.

What's the difference between announcers and actors?
There's no real difference. I believe that, in general, good actors are good voice-over actors. They can make a script come to life. In other words, they make me want to listen to what they're saying. I believe

that good announcers, who make up the majority of the voice-over recording world, are good actors as well. It's just not so obvious to us.

Can you tell us a little about how you work with talent and the difference between a union and nonunion process?
Most of the voice talent I get comes from the large talent agencies located in New York City, and about 90 percent of the casting we do is union. I request several people who I have worked with before and who fit the "specs" for the spot. My clients (the copywriters and producers from the ad agencies) want to hear anywhere between ten and thirty people auditioning for each role, depending on the script. That means that sometimes I have to call in more people than just the ones with whom I am familiar. Which is a good thing. It lets me get familiar with the new voices out there, and it gives my client more options in the end.

In fact, I am very open to meeting new talent. Sometimes I meet a voice-over talent who has been working in another part of the country and has just moved to New York. That has been one of the best parts of teaching at seminars for me: meeting new talent undiscovered by other casting agents. A far as demo reels go, I do what I can to listen to them. I have probably listened to more than a thousand in the past year. But even though in this business the focus is on the voice, there is something about meeting someone face to face and getting a sense of how they approach a piece of ad copy. The unsolicited demo reel is probably my least favorite way of finding talent.

I get nonunion people from various sources, depending on the jobs: talent agents who specialize in nonunion talent; people I have met while teaching (seminars or privately); recommendations from voice-over teachers; comedians or actors whom I have seen performing around town; acting organizations like Actor's Equity.

In general, union talent is more professional and less freaked out to be auditioning. Nonunion talent is greener, but sometimes, depending on what you're doing, that nervousness and realness can be a good thing.

Any pet peeves about voice actors?

Wow. Um. Not asking questions about the script because they don't want to embarrass themselves. I think that asking questions shows that you care about your read. Ask away!

Being late for a booking! The client is paying a fortune for studio time.

Staying after the audition. We are usually on a strict timetable. So be ready when your name is called, and be ready to leave when you're done so we can get to the next person.

Bookings

13

- The recording session
- What to do after the recording session
- Voice for Hire: Joe Cipriano

Congratulations. You booked a spot! That's something to be very proud of. It might have taken six months or a year to get there, but you beat out your competition.

You probably got the booking after your agent sent you out on an audition. You did your read. You were then officially "on hold," meaning you had been selected by the client to be on a short list of voice artists, one of whom would ultimately record the spot. You got the call and you got the appointment time. Or you may have gotten the booking without an audition. A client may have heard you on voice123.com, voicehunter.com, or www.voices.com and hired you through the site. You may also have gotten the booking directly from your reel. Peter became the voice of all of the promos for "Dora the Explorer's Live Tour," based on the popular children's television show, directly from a mailing he did to a personal contact at Clear Channel. The contact forwarded Peter's reel to his boss, who was impressed by how well Peter's range and vocal qualities suited the reads. The client saw no need to hold auditions and asked him to record the job. This became a lucrative, ongoing gig.

Typically, most voice-over bookings take place a few days after auditions have been held and the voice talents have been selected— spots are recorded and produced quickly so that they can be broadcast in a timely manner. Most commercials and promos take approximately one hour to record. Narrations can take several weeks, if not months, depending upon the amount of material involved.

THE RECORDING SESSION

If, like Randy, you don't live in Los Angeles, New York, or Chicago, you will record from your home studio or from a recording studio in your area. In both places the client will hear you through a phone patch or ISDN and give direction. If you're recording via ISDN in a studio, an engineer will handle the technical aspects of the recording, including timing the spot.

If you live in Los Angeles, New York, or Chicago, you will most likely be asked to arrive at a recording facility and to wait in the lounge before entering the studio. Frequently, recording sessions for a number of projects are scheduled back to back, so time is of the essence. It's always a good idea to arrive early for a booking, so you have time to relax, gather your thoughts, and enter the studio ready to work.

> "Don't be afraid to make an ass out of yourself. For some of us this is really easy. Let it all hang out."
>
> —Michael Sheehy, voice artist

In most cases, a director, a producer, a recording engineer, a copywriter, and even the client (be it McDonald's, AT&T, or Crest) will be in a room on the other side of the glass. You will be asked to enter the studio, put on the headphones, and communicate with one indi-vidual who speaks for the entire group. While it can be nerve-racking to be watched and listened to by a group, try not to find the situation intimidating. Your audience is rooting for you and is on your side. You have already been chosen to represent a client/product/service to the public, so take that validation with you into the booth each and every time you book a spot. With that said, always be polite and eager to learn.

It is not unheard of to record a spot fifty to a hundred times to give the producer and engineer what they are looking for. In post-production, they will select the best parts of each of the scripts/takes that you recorded and edit them together with seamless transitions, making your recordings sound like one complete read. In many instances, you will be asked to do "pick-ups" on a specific line or segment of dialogue—slightly varied readings, one of which the editor will piece into the final spot in post-production.

At times during a booking, the production team will play back what you just recorded. Yes, they are discussing your reads, but be patient and try not to become paranoid. They may ask you again to read the line with a variation in direction. Sometimes direction can be very technical and involve fine points of pacing, diction, volume, microphone levels, and placement. At other times, the direction may be intended to hone your creative presentation.

If you book a multiple-person spot, you may record your dialogue without the other actor(s) present. This makes the voice actor's job more challenging, but the magic takes place in post-production when the engineer combines the isolated dialogue pick-ups and puts them together, creating a seamless and timeless conversation. It's a bit like acting on a film set in front of a green screen, reacting to something or someone that doesn't exist until special effects are implemented.

Take It Again!

It is not uncommon for a booking to take twenty minutes or less. This indicates the team had a clear idea of what they wanted and you delivered it in a few takes. Most voice-over artists playing at a major level and doing studio work can get the job done in the second, third, or fourth takes. (But if they have not "nailed" it at that point, they go through as many takes as necessary to please the client.)

More than once we have had the experience of being in a recording session with a producer or client who had absolutely no idea what he or she wanted. Occasionally, after twenty-five or so takes, a savvy engineer will say, "Hey, listen to this take," and play it. The client says, "Yes! That's the one!" only to find out that it was the second or third take you recorded.

Regardless of how few or how many takes you record within the first hour of your booking, by the terms of your contract you will be paid your hourly rate. If the recording stretches into a second hour, even by a minute or so, you are entitled to be paid for a second hour of booking time.

Tips for a Great Recording Session

Here's what a couple of pros say about the recording experience.

Don't be afraid to make an ass out of yourself. For some of us this is really easy. Let it all hang out. It is much easier for a director to pull you back in than to stand behind you, prodding you forward. Go for it!

Be on time. Be an hour early rather than a minute late. The director, producer, and other professionals have a schedule, too.

Make the experience pleasant. There's more to life than news, weather, and sports. Don't think that going in and reading the copy is enough. A little schmoozing never hurts. You don't have to be a kiss-ass, but be real, leave them with a good feeling, wanting to work with you again.

Try to discover what the writer is saying. Don't apply the copy to you . . . apply yourself to the copy. What's the point? How can you best get it across?

—Michael Sheehy

Prepare. That's the most important thing. Don't go into the studio with an unmarked script; really saturate yourself with what's there. Even read things about the subject. Something will happen inside you if you prepare and are really into the copy. Don't just think of the voice . . . think of the material, too. I think the most important things are to be prepared and to be professional. Don't go into the studio and tell jokes. Somebody is paying for that studio—get in, do your job as best you can, and get out.

—Peter Thomas

AFTER THE RECORDING SESSION

If you belong to a union, the first thing you should do at the end of the recording session is sign the job sheet. If you are nonunion, you should present an invoice. Voice actors sometimes make arrangements to be paid on the spot, but otherwise you can expect to be paid thirty days from the date of recording. Any longer is unacceptable, unless different terms of payment are dictated in your contract with the client or agency. If you are working from home and delivering the audio via e-mail, you can ask to be paid by PayPal or some other online instant payment method.

Ask the production team for the phone number and e-mail address of a contact from whom you can obtain a copy of the fully produced spot. You want to have copies of all recorded voice-over work for your own archives. You may want to use this spot to replace an older spot or a mock spot on your demo reel. In any case, it's always good to keep your work on file. Wait at least a week before making the request. In many instances, you may find it difficult to obtain a recording of your session, but persist until you get what you want, without being pushy.

Consider yourself a success if you have made a professional impression on the company and production team with whom you have just worked. A positive first experience will make it more likely that they will think of you in the future for additional voice-over work.

Voice for Hire: Joe Cipriano

My first job was working on the air at the age of sixteen at WWCO in Waterbury, Connecticut. Then I moved to Washington, D.C., in 1975 to take a radio job with NBC. They owned two stations in the nation's capital at the time, and I was hired to host the midday show on WKYS 93.9 FM. I replaced Willard Scott, who was moving on to do the weather reporting full time for NBC's WRC TV-4. I was a kid and he was a seasoned pro. I spent a week with Willard while he did his last radio shows, and he showed me the ropes of the station. I got to know Willard pretty well during my three years at NBC and learned a lot from him. Humility and kindness toward others were the top two lessons, followed closely by not taking yourself too seriously. I would marvel at his ability to remember the names of everyone in the building. He was the highlight of everyone's day at the station and was famous for giving every woman he passed in the halls a kiss on the forehead. I learned there are two ways you can go in a career and in life—the "it's all about me" route or the "we're all in this together" route. In broadcasting or voice-over you will come across the egotistical, cynical, prima donna, angry types and the down-to-earth, happy-in-their-own-skin types. I chose the latter, and yes, I think it's a conscious decision.

My wife, Ann, and I decided to move to Los Angeles because we were both in broadcasting (she was a TV news writer and producer) and we knew the big jobs were there. Since my goal was working in TV and movie voice-overs, Los Angeles was the place to be.

> "A casting person can smell desperation as soon as you walk in the door, and it's not a pleasant smell."
>
> —Joe Cipriano, promo announcer

By the way, I have a rule . . . never quit a job and move to a new city without having a job waiting for you there. There are too many talented people here in Los Angeles trying to make it in Hollywood. You have a much better chance of making it if you are not struggling just to eat and keep a roof over your head. Being a starving actor is not as romantic as it may sound when famous celebrities talk about their early years. Just ask any starving actor.

A casting person can smell desperation as soon as you walk in the door, and it's not a pleasant smell. Who would you rather hang with, someone who is racked with desperation, paranoia, and bitterness or someone who is calm, cool, and confident? Desperation is not your friend in an audition situation, while confidence ups your chances and is a sure sign of a winner.

So, while I desperately wanted to move to Los Angeles, I didn't make the move until I had a job lined up (a "day job," so to speak) that would take care of the rent and living expenses while I pursued my dream of doing voice-overs. The "day job" was another radio gig. Part of my job at the radio station was dubbing commercials. Each commercial came into the station on reel-to-reel tape from an ad agency or recording studio. I wrote down the name and address of each one and sent my demo tape to them that night.

Once I started to get work in voice-overs I continued to work in radio as well. I didn't want to give up the "day job" just yet. In fact, I continued doing both until 1992, even though I had been working every day as a voice-over artist since 1988. I finally gave up my radio because between the two jobs, I was working seven days a week and I felt relatively certain that voice-overs had become a steady income. But to this day, I haven't given up the concept of having several different jobs at one time. I still do some part-time radio, and I take on local radio and TV voice-over jobs because they are usually contract jobs that guarantee a certain amount of dollars and a set term of employment. A voice-over career is constantly changing. You lose a gig here, you gain a gig there. It's good to have a lot of balls in the air, so to speak, so that when you lose one you still have plenty of others to juggle.

I guess the first time I thought I had really accomplished something was when I did the trailers and TV commercials for *Fast Times at Ridgemont High* in 1982. It wasn't a career maker, but it was a hint that I could actually work in this field. My next biggest moment—the real life changer—was getting hired by the Fox network in 1988 as their promo voice. It was a bigger gig than I ever dreamed of landing, and it brought me unimaginable opportunities and rewards.

In my opinion, you have to work hard at your dream . . . put in at least an hour a day every single day toward moving your voice-over career forward. I think you can focus more on your dream if you have a job that's bringing in the bread and butter. Stay positive, work hard, and use the confidence in yourself and your accomplishments both in voice-over and in your "day job" to keep yourself moving forward.

Home Studios and Technology

14

- Setting up a studio
- Basic considerations
- Beginner, mid-range, and high-end studios
- Studios of the Pros
- Voice for Hire: Brian Lee

More and more voice actors are working from home studios. We can't quite make the statement that, in today's digital world, if you don't have a home studio you might as well forget about a career in voice-over. Even with the technology to prepare and send voice-over samples and auditions to casting directors, agents, marketing companies, and, of course, the highly prized paying client, the most important tools for a successful voice artist are still talent, training, and the ability to interpret and read copy. The fact remains, however, that in today's high-tech environment, a well-equipped home studio significantly augments the more essential elements of a successful voice-over career.

SETTING UP A STUDIO

The first step in building a home studio is to consider the basic equipment you'll need, as well as power requirements, air-conditioning, and wiring from the studio to the outside world. These basic considerations include:

- Adequate power and a backup power system for all computers and audio hardware.
- An air-conditioning system that utilizes large ductwork to eliminate the air noise created by grills and dampers. The air-conditioning system should be slightly oversized to maintain a constant cool temperature in a room where a substantial amount of equipment generates heat.

Randy's Home Studio

My first studio was in a guest bedroom. I hung a rug on the wall and placed my microphone, a Shure SM7, in front of it, to eliminate any sound reflection. I used a Symetrix EQ, a Mackie mix pad, a DAT machine (to record and playback audio), and a CD burner.

When I moved I decided to create a better studio. Among other improvements, I wanted the ability to edit my own audio so my clients would no longer have to hear mistakes and the inevitable fuh-fumps. With a stroke of the keyboard, I roll my recording program and can see what the voice print looks like, making it easy to locate the breaths and inevitable mouth noise that can happen when we enunciate.

My current studio is state of the art. Under the supervision of Wayne Dillon of Envision Theater, I created a 6-by-9 soundproof booth, sparing no expense to create the ultimate voice-tracking environment. The booth has a dropped ceiling and sound-reinforced walls with a carpet over a cement floor. I special-ordered a steel-reinforced door with a window from Acoustic Systems. The door weighs more than three hundred pounds and, when shut, creates a vacuum in the booth,

---

- Wiring to accommodate phone lines, special circuits like DSL, cable, ISDN, and other data circuits as they come on the scene (for example, fiber optics).
- Enough space to accommodate the use of several microphones simultaneously (when microphones are placed too close to one another interference can occur).

The Beginner Studio

Basic equipment is required if you want to digitally record and send auditions to a casting person or client. A basic studio setup will work for recording some jobs, but for others that require high-quality audio, you will likely need to use a local studio. A beginner studio with the equipment listed below can cost as little as $200, assuming you already have a computer. You'll need a computer; a USB microphone; an editing program; a CD burner, and acoustics for sound control. At the beginner

providing maximum protection from sounds in the outside world. The booth walls are covered in dark gray foam core with light gray sound panels for accent.

I work standing, so I had a stand-up board built, and I can also use a counter-height bar stool to sit comfortably. I have two microphones, a Sennheiser MKH416 shotgun, with a popper stopper, that is run though an Avalon pre-amp, and a Manley Reference Cardioid Microphone paired with a Manley Voxbox combo. The combination of mic and pre-amp is perfect for my tones.

On my stand-up workspace is a Mac monitor, a Mackie mix pad, and a few photos and personal items for inspiration. In the studio office I share with my husband, I have a G-4 (as a backup), a Mac Pro 2.66 Dual Core with M-Box, an Avalon pre-amp, a Telos One digital phone hybrid, a Telos XStream (ISDN codec), a Tascam CD RW 700, a Radix 1600 Distribution Amplifier, and Event 20/20 Studio monitors. I use a Furman power conditioner so I can shut down everything with one switch. I have installed a generator made by Superior Power Systems that runs by propane gas; a 1,000-gallon propane tank is buried in my yard, so in case of a hurricane or violent storm (common in Florida) I am ready to work anytime.

---

stage, you will likely want a USB microphone that can plug directly into your computer; popular models are the Rode Podcaster (around $250) and the Blue Snowball (around $100).

The Mid-Range Studio

A mid-range studio will serve the part-time to full-time professional voice artist. With this setup, you will be able to record professional, high-quality audio. This studio can run anywhere from $1,500 to $7,000, depending on the quality of equipment you purchase. You'll need a computer; a microphone; headphones; an editing program; a mic pre-amp; a mixing board; a CD burner; acoustics for sound control, and appropriate cabling. A mid-range studio might have a Shure SM7A, a classic radio announcer mic that is highly reliable and costs around $375. Another classic, the EV RE20, goes for around $400.

A High-End Studio

Equipment for a high-end recording studio, including an ISDN codec, is more sophisticated and more expensive. The ISDN codec (see page TK) enables you to dial in to any other studio and record with the highest audio quality. You must have this type of studio if you plan to make voice-over a full-time career. For a high-end studio, you'll need a computer; a microphone; headphones; studio monitors; an editing program; a mic pre-amp; an ISDN codec; a mixing board; a CD burner; an FTP site (see below); acoustics for sound control, and appropriate cabling. A high-end studio might have a Neumann BCM-104 mic, which runs around $1,000. The ever-popular Sennheiser MKH416, a common fixture in many high-end studios, costs around $1,300.

EQUIPMENT: THE DETAILS

Here's a closer look at the equipment that you'll want to consider for your home studio.

Computer

You can work with any kind of computer, but, obviously, sound is a key factor for a voice artist. PC tower-style computers usually have loud fans that can bleed into open mics. Laptops or Macs are quieter, as their fans turn on only when they are working hard. If you are using a PC tower, consider an isolation box such as the ones manufactured by Acoustilock. This noise solution starts at about $1,200 and is very effective. You can also place a physical divider, called a Gobo, between your computer and the microphone setup to provide an extra level of isolation.

Audio files can be very large, so you will need sufficient memory. You also might want to consider purchasing an external hard drive to back up your files.

Microphone

Of all the equipment you will consider, the microphone will have the most direct impact on the sound of your recordings, so you must be diligent in your research and find the right mic for you. Types include USB, condenser, dynamic, solid state, and tube, to name a few. The mic that works best for you is a personal preference, so our best suggestion is to go a dealer and try several. Most good dealers will let you leave a deposit and take a few mics home to compare them.

Each microphone has different sound quality. Depending on the sound of your voice, different styles of microphone may accent the overarching tones in your voice, or make your voice bassey and larger than life, or make it sound bright or strident or neutral and boring. A more expensive mic is not necessarily the one that will make your voice sound best. Record the same read with several different mics, and you should be able to pick the one that is the most flattering to your voice and the way you want it to sound.

The microphones described below differ mainly in the way they are connected to your computer or studio, the way they are powered, and the types of components they utilize.

- USB: This is the least expensive microphone and the easiest to use. You simply connect the microphone to the computer via a USB port. You do not need additional power, as the microphone draws its power through the USB connection.
- Dynamic: This type is widely used for many applications on stage and in the studio. Dynamic mics do not require additional power, but you will need to use a microphone pre-amp (see page 150) to send a loud and full signal into the mixing equipment.
- Condenser: The condenser microphone requires additional power, usually provided by battery. The condenser mic may also use a power supply known as phantom power, applied by a button on your mic pre-amp. You can damage your equipment by applying phantom power to mics that do not require it, so always follow the manufacturer's instructions carefully.
- Tube: A tube microphone usually provides a warm and smooth tone, which results from the addition of a vacuum tube, much like those found in guitar amplifiers and other audio equipment.
- Solid state: This high-end mic provides a sound similar to the one you get with a tube mic, but it does not have a vacuum tube inside.

You can place your mic on a stand or on a boom. Make sure that the mic is stable on a stand. Leave enough space for a copy stand directly under the mic so that you can read the copy comfortably while speaking directly into the mic. If you are using a boom stand or a heavy mic, position a small weight over one of the legs of the mic stand, to keep your mic from falling over. Once the mic is firmly in place, connect it to your mixer or sound interface with the accompanying cable; most mics call for an XLR cable.

Headphones

While studio headphones vary considerably in quality and price, you can buy a perfectly acceptable pair for a home studio for around $80 to $100. Test out a few in the store to find the style you prefer. We suggest buying a pair with ample cushioning around the earphones to prevent external noise from entering the headset.

Studio Monitors

A wide variety of affordable studio monitors, the speakers used in recording studios, is available for the home studio market. Prices for a pair of good monitors can range from a few hundred to a few thousand dollars. Try as many models as you can to find the speaker in your price range that sounds best.

Editing Program

Cost-saving solutions include the Garage Band software that comes free with new Mac computers, and Audacity, a free audio editing program for PCs that you can download from the Internet.

Many voice-over talents use Adobe Audition, which costs around $350, because it is easy to learn and use. Another option is the Digidesign M-Box Mini (around $350), which comes with Pro-Tools software; the industry standard, it allows you to edit more creatively than many similar programs do.

Mic Pre-Amp

A mic pre-amp has a number of functions, such as taking out sibilance with frequency (the highs you want to remove), squashing the signal to give you more "punch" and to keep the signal from over-modulating or breaking up, and adding high-end, mid-range, or low-end tones to your voice. Cut and boost controls are used to either cut out a frequency or to boost its level; they can also be used to dial out unwanted noise, such as that from an air-conditioner. Symetrix and DBX make a decent "mid-range" mic pre-amp. Avalon, Manley, and Focusrite are at the top end of the range.

ISDN Codec (and Other Up-and-Coming Options)

For most of us, ISDN stands for "I still don't know," although it is actually the acronym for Integrated Services Digital Network.

ISDN lines provide a way for a reading to be recorded with the highest quality, in any studio, anywhere in the world, simply by interfacing with the studio's ISDN phone lines and codec (the device that decodes the digital stream). Full-time professional voice artists use an ISDN codec, such as a Telos Zephyr, in their home studios.

This said, we should note that technology is changing all the time. Innovative software packages, such as SoundStreak, use the Internet to record and transfer audio, doing away with the need for expensive ISDN lines, hardware, subscription fees, and minute-by-minute line charges.

Mixing Board

The mixing board acts as a router and mixing device for many different sound sources. In a typical recording environment, a microphone is connected to a mic pre-amp and then connected to the mixing board. The mixing board gives additional signal controls before sending the sound to the monitors or computer. For most voice-over recordings you'll be doing from home, you will probably be able to get by with a smaller-scale mixing board.

FTP Site

If your files are too large to send easily, you will want to upload them to a File Transfer Protocol (FTP) site, from which files can be downloaded, and send your client a link. If you or your client do not have an FTP site, you can use one such as yousendit.com.

Steve Kamer's Home Studio

Steve Kamer is the voice of Inside Edition, *a syndicated King World daily entertainment show.*

I have a one-bedroom apartment, about 700 square feet. I made the bedroom into the studio and booth—when you walk into the bedroom, you think you're at a radio station. I've got a big console with a computer upfront, a telephone, speakers, a Zephyr, a phone hybrid, and a compressor; the room has been insulated so that it is the actual booth as well as the studio. I sit at the board and record my scripts either with the client on the line or unsupervised, working in an environment that is very comfortable.

I've hung insulated pads, like you see in a freight elevator or a moving van, from rods on the four largest walls. I cover the window with a specially made device—a piece of plywood, covered with burlap, that fits right into the window frame. I've covered the hardwood floor with carpeting and hung floor lamps and lights from a mike-boom type of arm.

My equipment is: a Sennheiser 416 mic, an Avalon 737 SP mic pre-amp, a vacuum tube, Apple G5 running Pro Tools, a DG 002 mixer, a Telos Zephyr XStream, a Telos One phone hybrid, a Samsung monitor, a pair of speakers by Gentech, and K240 headphones made by AKG, plus a pair of Sony headphones.

Noise/Sound Control

Your microphone can pick up equipment vibration that is transmitted through your walls, ceiling, or floor. If you don't have proper sound isolation, you will find yourself equalizing to overcome your studio's deficiencies and your microphone will not achieve the best sound. Remember: It is not only the microphone that makes your voice sound good; the environment surrounding the microphone is also a major factor.

While you won't be able to completely isolate your studio from the outside world, you can take measures to ensure a good recording environment. Situate the studio a good distance from any mechanical equipment that makes noise—air-conditioners, washers, dryers, computer printers, pool pumps, refrigerators with ice makers, as well as bathrooms, water pipes, and other plumbing. For the most sophisticated sound control, you can soundproof your walls, ceiling, and floors and install special doors and windows. Acoustical engineers can advise you on proper design and installation.

SO, AM I CHAINED TO MY STUDIO?

The answer is "No!" Voice artists need to travel occasionally to meet with their buyers and do the occasional session in person. You can use a studio in the location you are visiting or take your equipment with you. Many voice artists today use the Stone Booth in a Bag. This portable studio was designed by national voice artist Steve Stone and custom-built by Gretch-Ken Industries' GK Acoustics. The Stone Booth in a Bag is a three-sided, portable tabletop sound isolation enclosure, with an isolation curtain on the back side. The entire enclosure folds up into a custom-manufactured portable bag. Stone's mobile studio includes an Apple Powerbook G4 laptop, a Gliph PortaGig 80 gig external firewire hard drive, a Sennheiser MKH-416 microphone, a True Systems P-Solo Mic Pre, Digidesign's M-Box2 Mini, M-Audio IE-10 monitors, and a custom-made phone patch.

Technology, ever on the move, continues to make life easier for the voice artist—leaving us more time to perfect our craft.

Voice for Hire: Brian Lee

Brian Lee is a voice artist who, among many other gigs, tracks for *Tyra Banks* from his home studio in Florida.

Randy Thomas was using my studio to voice one of her TV clients while her Florida studio was being constructed, and she graciously dropped my name to Atlas Talent Agency. I was represented by a different New York talent agency at the time. Atlas was well versed in representing voice talent who lived outside of New York City and embraced the technology that enabled me to work from my studio in Florida. They were able to expose me to studios and networks that were comfortable using voice talent that they couldn't see in person.

Immediately after signing with Atlas, an opportunity to voice the *Connie Chung Show* on CNN came along. The agency called on a Friday at 6:00 P.M. and said, "Drop everything you're doing and do this audition." I voiced a single line, and emailed an mp3 file back. They called back about an hour later and informed me that I booked the gig, and that I had to start immediately. I was freaking out. In one hour, I went from voicing some television affiliates to voicing for a network. I had hit the big time. International exposure.

What's really changed the way we work is the method of delivery. We used to travel to a television station or a studio. Networks use to have booth announcers. A booth announcer usually had a single job . . . announcing for the network. Show up at 9:00 A.M., leave at 5:00 P.M. It was a single job. It's difficult to leave a building when you have to speak three times every hour. The creation of high-speed digital phone lines, the Internet, and computer-based digital audio recording/editing systems has certainly contributed to the success of almost every voice-over person on the planet. Audio can be recorded and delivered to virtually anywhere. So, instead of having a single announcing job at a television station or network or traveling around town to local studios, you can now stay in one location and work for anyone on earth. The invention of the digital network audio transceiver, which transmits and receives digital audio over ISDN lines (high-speed phone lines) has enabled us to be in one location and instantly connect anywhere in the world. This is what's changed everything. I live in Florida and work all over the world. One minute I'm on live with NBC in Los Angeles, the next minute, it's New York for the CBS Early Show. The whole time, I'm in Florida. The ability to make money is almost limitless. One of my biggest idols and inspirations, Joe Cipriano, has even worked live aboard a cruise ship in the middle of the open seas. Thank you technology. Many voice-over people don't have ISDN lines in their houses. You don't "have" to have it. Some clients who want live feeds may require it, and then you may be out of luck in that case. But really, for the most part, all you need is a computer with an audio recording/editing program and an Internet connection, a decent microphone, and above all, a quiet space to work. You can't have a loud-reflective room; you must have a space acoustically treated for voice, so there's not a bunch of echo when you speak.

Things have become a lot more portable now; laptops are a lot more powerful. I have a Mac that's only an inch thick and it has a recording/editing system on it and a very small interface that I can plug a microphone into. With the invention of wireless Internet, I can find a hot spot and just upload.

I think it's only going to get better. I think that technology is going to become so advanced that your microphone will be plugged into your computer or cell phone and you'll be able to sit in the middle of nowhere and have a live feed to anywhere in the world.

More Advice from the Pros

15

- Keys to success
- Seven P's for Perfection
- An Exercise from Debbie Ford

Peter has coached hundreds of voice-over artists . . . from highly successful actors, to writers, dancers, broadcasters, athletes, disc jockeys, and soccer moms. Peter's skill as a coach has as much to do with directing his talent in the booth as it does with helping people live the life of a voice-over artist outside the booth.

This field is not for the fainthearted. There are great rewards (artistic, as well as monetary) that come with being a professional voice-over artist, and yet there are challenges to be faced along the way, as there are in any profession. It takes time, perseverance, persistence, and realistic goals to establish yourself.

Every successful voice-over artist we have interviewed for this book has had his or her own journey. When you look at those who are successful, you learn that success is very subjective and seemingly random at times. Let's face it: You have to be a little bit crazy and more than a little adventurous to want to map out a career in this industry.

SOME KEYS TO SUCCESS

We have witnessed a wide range of different paths to success, and we have also witnessed obvious paths that are likely to lead to failure. Those who have succeeded at voice-over did so because, first, they were able to function as people. Being successful alone will not complete you as a person; however, being a complete person will help you to succeed in whatever you try. Here are some general guidelines to help you be the voice-over artist you want to be.

Look into the Future

To truly be sure you are on the right path, take time to do the internal work that will clarify whether a career as a voice artist is the right choice for you. Find a quiet space and time, close your eyes, and imagine what your future will look like in a year, or two, or three. If you can see yourself using your voice as a creative expression of your personality, then you may be on the right path to realize your dreams.

Have a Safety Net

If you try to please others knowing that you are not honoring yourself and what you have to offer at your highest level, then your actions may prove to be self-destructive. Have you ever heard the expression, "Luck is where opportunity meets preparedness," or "I'd rather be lucky than smart"? Well, it turns out that to be successful in the world of voiceovers you need to be prepared, smart, talented, and lucky as well.

The best way to pursue a voice-over career is to have the security and financial backing of another endeavor. That safety net will help you bounce back after you've taken a few falls. It will prevent you from placing too much pressure on your voice-over career to pay the bills. If you are looking at voice-over as a means to pay for your lifestyle—including your mortgage or rent, car payments, and insurance—you are placing unrealistic demands on yourself to constantly book work. We're not discounting the thousands of people who make their living doing voice-over. However, these people did not start out as overnight successes. There is no such thing.

Handle Rejection

Voice-over is an art form and art is subjective. Therefore, one man's trash can be another man's treasure. Don't let outside influences shape your inner confidence. One casting director may love you and another may pay you no regard. That does not mean you are not valid; what it means is that people have individual preferences and tastes. This works in your favor—otherwise producers would hire the same voice-over artists time and time again and there would be no creative diversity.

The best voice-over artists are rejected dozens of times a week. This is because they audition dozens of times a week. Don't feel that you have to book 100 percent of the time, or anywhere near it. Instead, look at success as booking 1 percent of the time and auditioning a hundred times. The bottom line: When you don't book a job, don't let it rattle you. Let it fuel your desire to audition once again. In a business of numbers, the more auditions you have, the greater your chance of booking jobs. Remember, Babe Ruth had more home runs than any other baseball player of his time . . . but he also had a lot of strikeouts.

Handle Success

Be open to success, and trust that if you are truly committed to your path and have some talent and a tremendous amount of focus and drive, the universe will present you with a small miracle—success, based on your ability to use your voice effectively and your professional knowledge of a competitive marketplace. How you use your success will be up to you.

There's a practical side to success, too. For those of you who are currently earning your keep as voice-over artists, be mindful that your career may sometimes falter. Quite often, these things are completely out of your control. For instance, Peter had a client who booked a national campaign for a well-known product. As a result, this artist earned hundreds of thousands of dollars in a relatively short period of time. He splurged on fancy cars, a New York City apartment, fine dining, and travel. All of this seemed affordable at the time. What he did not realize was that every campaign ends, and when it ends, the money stops coming in. Needless to say, once the campaign ended he could no longer afford this high-rolling lifestyle.

Unfortunately, this is an all-too-common scenario for voice-over artists who strike it rich early and easily. So if you should book lucrative work—ad campaigns, promo contracts, narration contracts, an animated series—always reinvest some of your earnings back into your business, and budget with the knowledge that every job is finite. If you do not already have a financial adviser, get one who can steer you toward smart and safe investments.

The Intangible Factors

Finally, here are some pearls of wisdom that could advance your voice-over career:

- Producers want to work with people who are generally nice to work with.
- Be open to suggestions and critique. No one wants to work with someone who becomes defensive and off-putting.
- Don't be desperate. This is easily telegraphed and a client will lose confidence in you if you come across as needy and insecure.
- Don't underestimate your value.
- Don't overestimate your value either. Nobody wants to work with someone with an inflated ego.
- Don't let personal problems or issues in your life affect the work you do.
- Be open to refining your skills at all times throughout your career. You can never learn enough.
- Be punctual. In fact, be early.
- Don't judge yourself too hard.
- Never take any of your success for granted.

AN EXERCISE FROM DEBBIE FORD

We all get off track once in a while. When Randy loses her focus, she turns to an amazing support team of highly gifted coaches, one of whom is Debbie Ford.

Here is an exercise you can do if you need to identify why something is happening within you that is causing you to feel scared. Debbie's exercise can help you identify what you are feeling, embrace it, and change the voice of fear into the voice of power! Take a moment to get yourself comfortable. Close your eyes, and address the following as honestly as you can.

State Your Cherished Goal

Think about one of your important goals.

The Voice for Hire Seven *P*'s for Perfection!

1. **Be practical.** Have a goal, articulate it carefully, study it, read about it and study some more, then give it time and money. A career takes years to create, so don't give up your "day job" too soon. Practice and patience pay off.

2. **Be prepared.** Study and learn from the best. Then invest in a great demo, as well as presentable and professional branding and artwork. Always show up ready to work. Bring with you every-thing you have learned and practiced, then let it go and be in the moment. Remember, you never get a second chance to make a first impression.

3. **Be positive.** Nothing sends a dream crashing and burning faster than a negative attitude. People can feel fear and self-loathing, and they flee from it as though from a house on fire.

Identify the Voice of Fear

What does the voice of the fear that stands as an obstacle to attaining this goal sound like? Is it a whisper? Is it a shout? On a scale of 1 to 10, is it a 10 or is it a 1?

Call forward the voice of your fears. What does it say to you? Does it tell you that you can't do it on your own, you can't teach an old dog new tricks, you don't have the right education?

See the Underlying Fear

Now, let's see if a deeper fear lies beneath these fears. Ask the voice of fear to tell you what the underlying fear is. Does it say you're really not talented enough, one day everyone will find out the truth about you, you've been lucky so far but your luck is running out?

Uncover the Lie

The voice that has been abusing you, the voice of self-doubt and fear, needs to be uncovered. You need to discover that your fear is a lie. How old do you think this fear is? Ask that fear, What do you need from me? What do you need to have peace right now? What do you

4. **Be professional.** Be available (if a client needs you, never say no), be on time; even better, be early. Respect your coach, casting director, client, agent, or anyone you interface with. Show them you are a professional by getting down to business as soon as they indicate they are ready for you. To repeat: Always be available. This is how many of us in this business get jobs . . . another person is not available and we are.

5. **Be persistent.** Never say never! Don't let one negative response upset your vision of where you are going. If you think you have what it takes to be successful, then persevere. Persistence pays off!

6. **Be powerful.** Show up as you at your best and your highest expression of who you are.

7. **Be phenomenal.** You have permission to be all and everything you want to be. If you are following all the steps above and your intention is clear, you have permission to be the remarkable talent you envision yourself to be. You are unique, and that is extraordinary.

need to know? What do you need me to do to take care of you? Ask the fear what it is it looking for: encouragement, support, kindness, compassion, understanding, integrity, safety?

Listen for the Voice of Faith

The voice of faith is spirit—or you may think of it as the God force, or an infinite power. It whispers in your ear, saying "There's something bigger and better waiting for you."

Imagine that the voice of faith has one strong message, and all the others are just messages on top of that core message. What is the core message? Is it that you can do whatever you want, that you inspire people, that your contribution matters, that God has a plan for you? What does the voice of faith want you to hear or want you to know? Write it down.

Your Practice for Remembering Faith

Now, let's ask the voice of faith what practice you could put in place to ensure you really listen to the voice. You may need to surround yourself with certain words by writing them down and keeping them on top of your desk, in your car, in your kitchen. Or maybe you need to make an audio recording in your own voice, telling yourself the words you need to hear, and listen to that for a couple of minutes each day. Record it in the third person or in the first person, whatever is most effective for you. For example:

"Stacey is a superstar. People look up to her and admire her," or

"I am a superstar. People look up to me and admire me."

Make a commitment to listen to the voice of faith and thank it for sharing its loving wisdom with you.

Neutralize Fear

Once you distinguish the voice of fear and determine how long you've been carrying it, your next job is to neutralize it. The healthy part of you needs to say, "Hey, I know you're scared—and that's okay. Good for you that you're trying something new. Good for you that you're willing to be open to that next level of success."

If you've got fear, and the voice of fear is going crazy, just saying, "I'm great, I'm pretty . . . " is probably not going to work. It will be much more effective to identify and acknowledge the voice of fear: "Wow, there's the voice of fear! I'm really feeling scared today. You know, I'm going to take really good care of myself, and the part of me that's scared today."

Stopping the Internal War, Coming into Alignment

Our unconscious is the director of our lives, whether we're aware of it or not. Your conscious mind might say, "My goal is have this great success." But your unconscious commitment may be not be more successful than your brother. You'll always have the internal war going on. You must tend to these unresolved issues and address the fears that you have in order to see a bigger vision. With that vision in place, you'll be able to align your unconscious with your conscious, and your desires will unfold in the external world.

EPILOGUE

THE LAST TAKE

One of the most successful and generous voice-over artists I have known is Don LaFontaine (who wrote the foreword to this book). I met Don for the first time in 1993 when I was still a DJ on The Wave 94.7 in Los Angeles. The radio station was at that time on the fifth floor of the FOX Broadcast Center. I had become good friends with Dave Jacobs, one of the room producers, and he invited me to sit in when Don came in to read his Fox promos. This was just one of Don's many stops during the day.

I sat in awe listening to Don as he read in that instantly recognizable voice. "In a world. . . ." I was in heaven. He nailed the program promotional spot in one take. Before he left they asked—no, pleaded—with him to find time in his day to come back and do another promo and some tags.

I was told later that Don would allow people who wanted to become voice-over artists to ride with him in his limousine and see what it is like to be Don LaFontaine for a day. I was on the phone instantly calling Steve Tisherman, Don's agent, asking him if I could spend the day with Don.

I received a call the next day giving me directions to Don's house and the time I should arrive. Don's day started at NBC and from there he proceeded around town to the other networks and trailer houses. Don still works a lot and earns a very healthy living, but he does not need to get into his limo as often because of recording technology that allows him to work from home.

Don is one of those generous actors who share their experience with others who want to learn the ropes. He sets an example: Those of us who are in the enviable business of voice-overs, loving what we do every day, must reach out and extend a hand to people who want to learn how to do this work. I believe that our purpose in life is to learn how to love ourselves and others, to love what we do and do it gloriously, and then find a way to give back. If you are living a full life that consists of doing what you love every day, then you are truly blessed.

It is this belief that led me to become a teacher, and I am so grateful to be able to help young men and women along the way.

—Randy

As an artist, I have been blessed on two fronts. One, I've been getting paid to flex the creative partnership of mind and muscle as a voice artist for more than twenty years. Two, I have found a second career I never planned on: developing and showcasing other talented artists.

I have been fortunate enough to work with some of the brightest and most gifted people in the world, and I take more pride in their growth as artists than in my own endeavors.

The funny thing is that my students have taught *me* how to be a better artist, and the experience is one I hope never ends.

This book has given me the opportunity to reach out on a broader level to artists everywhere, who are as eager and committed to explore a new craft or to hone a familiar one as the artists who walk into my studio every day of the week.

Okay, so maybe I'm blessed on three fronts.

—Peter

GLOSSARY

ABC read: As in "Give me an ABC on the last line." Reading the line or lines three times in a row with various inflections or interpretations so as to give the producer three different choices.

Alt: For "alternate," a variation of the copy.

Alt take: A variation of the reading or performance.

Analog(ue): Audio or video created in an analog or linear format; nondigital.

Animatic: A way of testing a concept with the potential audience before the actual shooting of a spot.

Animation: A movie or cartoon consisting of a series of drawn, painted, or computer-generated scenes.

Animation actor: The person hired to voice-over the animation.

Announcer: The informational voice-over in a script. Sometimes referred to in the copy as ANN.

Audio booth: Enclosure with a microphone where the voice-over performance is recorded.

Audio sweetening: The process of adding the voice-over to picture.

Audition: The process in which an actor tries out for a particular role.

Booking: Being hired for a job.

Breakdown: The description provided by the client as to what kind of voice talent or read they are looking for.

Buy: When the producer/director is happy with a particular read they say, "That's a buy."

Callback: Being requested to return for another time; moving on to the next level after a good audition; getting one step closer to final selection.

Cans: Headphones.

Casting: The process of auditioning ("reading") various talent for a particular role or job.

Clean contract: Requesting rights in a contract to be unlimited.

Clean take: One that is free of noise or ambient sound.

Copy: The printed material or script you read from.

Copywriter: The person or persons responsible for writing the copy.

Credit: Recognition of your contribution to a particular spot or program.

Cue: The signal given to begin a performance.

Digital: Audio or video that is nonlinear. Transmitting, representing, editing, or storing data in the form of binary digits, as in a computer.

Digital recording: A form of audio recording in which sounds are stored as numbers, producing a more noise-free sound.

Digital television: Television broadcasting in which the picture is transmitted as a digital signal that is decoded by a device in or attached to the viewer's television set.

Digitize: The process of taking an analog audio/video source and transferring it via an analog-to-digital converter into an editing program or device.

Donut: Style of commercial where the copy is inserted between music or another voice-over, e.g., music jingle to open the spot, announcer copy in the middle followed by the jingle to close out the spot.

Freelance: Not bound by a particular agent or contract.

FTP Server: An FTP server is a software application running the File Transfer Protocol (FTP), which is the protocol for exchanging files over the Internet.

HFC: Short for Hybrid Fiber Co-ax, a way of delivering video, voice telephony, data, and other interactive services over coaxial and fiber optic cables.

ISDN: Abbreviation for Integrated Services Digital Network, an international communications standard for sending voice, video, and data over digital telephone lines or normal telephone wires. ISDN supports data transfer rates of 64 Kbps (64,000 bits per second).

MP3: The name of the file extension and also the name of the type of file for MPEG, audio layer 3. Layer 3 shrinks the original sound data from a CD without sacrificing sound quality. MP3 files, because they are small in size, can easily be transferred across the Internet.

Phone patch: The ability to allow someone to listen in on a record session via the phone line.

Pick-up: When the actor is asked to reread a line or series of lines in a spot or scene. This can be done during the session or in a subsequent session.

Plus Ten: The amount paid to the agent for the handling or negotiating of a booking that is sometimes added to the gross paid for by the client or buyer.

Residuals: Money paid periodically to the performer for the continued use of his work product.

Scale: The rate set by the unions as the price for a specific type or recording or job. Other relevant terms are above scale (more than) and below scale (less than).

Slate: The act of identifying yourself and/or the product at the start of recording.

SOT: Sound on tape. The sound bites that are excerpted and placed within a news story, promo, or narration. The announcer's voice-over is generally placed on either or both sides of the SOT.

Take: A single pass at a particular reading of copy. Recordings are generally done in a series of takes.

10 percent: The amount charged to the talent by the agents for the handling of a particular booking or job. This amount comes out of the talent's gross pay.

Unions: An organization of wage earners that is set up to serve and advance its members interests in terms of wages, benefits, and working conditions. The unions that represent working voice-over actors are the American Federation of Television and Radio Artists (AFTRA) and the Screen Actors Guild (SAG).

Some Telephone-Specific Terminology

ACD: For Automated Call Distributor. This system answers and delivers a single message like "all lines are busy" and places the call on hold. Then, as representatives become available, the system evenly distributes them to the available reps.

Automated attendant: A replacement for the receptionist. It plays a greeting and offers the caller a choice to direct the path of their call.

Digital announcer: A piece of equipment that plays a message back once or continuously.

On hold message: The messages that play while calls are holding. Usually this is voice and music together.

Telephony: This is the most widely used term to describe all services and equipment used for voice message with telephones.

Text to speech application: A software application that "sees" the written word and actually "speaks" the text as hearable audio. Used in some systems to read e-mail messages back over the phone.

Voice mail: This is a basic service that plays a greeting—most times in the recipient's own voice—plays a beep, and records a message. Some new systems display the message in a visual format that can be played on a computer screen or as an e-mail attachment. This also means it can be forwarded to e-mail accounts.

SOURCES AND CONTRIBUTORS

J. J. Adler, agent, Abrams Artists Agency

Mark Avery, voice-over talent

Michael Bell, voice-over talent

John Biffar, filmmaker and owner Dreamtime Productions,
    Fort Myers, Florida

Gil Cates, producer

Stephanie Ciccarelli, owner of voices.com

Joe Cipriano, voice-over talent

Jen Cohn, voice-over talent

David Coleman, owner of SoundStreak, Inc.

Wayne Dillon, Audio Engineer and co-owner of Idea Garden
    Advertising, Vero Beach, Florida

Ryan Fagman, audio engineer at PDR Voice Over Coaching

Debbie Ford, *New York Times* best-selling author, educator, and
    founder of the Ford Institute for Integrative Coaching at
    JFK University

Patrick Fraley, voice-over talent

Anne Gartlan, voice-over talent

Andy Geller, voice-over talent

Vanessa Gilbert, agent and partner, TGMD Talent Agency

Marc Graue, owner, Marc Graue Recording Studio in Burbank,
    California

Jennifer Hale, voice-over talent

Claudia Howard, Recorded Books, Inc.

Steve Kamer, voice-over talent

Brian Lee, voice-over talent

Lisa Marber-Rich, agent and partner, Atlas Talent Agency

Tony Mennuto, Creative Director of Sound Lounge

Mike Pollock, voice-over talent

Jamie Rosenberg, greatdividestudios.com in Aspen, Colorado

John Shanahan, creator and former owner of Hooked on Phonics

Michael Sheehy, voice-over talent

Peter Thomas Sr., voice-over talent

Marice Tobias, master voice-over coach

Keri Tombazian, voice-over talent

Alex Torrenegra, cofounder of voice123.com

Billy Vera, voice-over talent

Jonn Wasser, agent and partner, Atlas Talent Agency

Randy West, voice-over talent

Barry Zate, voice-over talent and owner of IMAGE Teleproducts

INDEX